'O'Siadhail gives us a double feast. First, PSALTER unites lyrical, beautifully crafted poetry with deep, urgent and questioning love of God and of life. Then GOSPEL gently and perceptively draws us into the stories of Jesus. The combination opens up a way of wise faith and mature love, alert to both the personal and the public challenges of our time'.

—**David F. Ford**, *Regius Professor of Divinity Emeritus, University of Cambridge*

'Many devotional poets have explored the great lyric themes of love, age, nature, art and loss. Few have had as much fun in the process as O'Siadhail. Tender, exuberant and physical, these poems celebrate the richness and variety of an inner life focused on spiritual experience, within a consciousness that also "cannot get enough of earthly things". This is a joyous collection, full of energy, self-acceptance and hope'.

—**Hazel Hutchison**, *Professor of English Literature, University of Leeds*

'Love and prayer are the intertwined themes of every poem in this book, which demonstrates that praising God well is less a spontaneous act than the work of a lifetime spent in faith. O'Siadhail shares the Psalmists' unapologetic subjectivity, the immediacy of their prayer, their insistence on the actuality of a loving relationship with God, perceived in part through suffering. Here the mature poet prays for "years to leave love's legacy behind", and this book is part of the fulfillment of his wise desire'.

—**Ellen F. Davis**, *Amos Ragan Kearns Distinguished Professor of Bible and Practical Theology, Duke Divinity School*

'After the brilliant inventiveness and seminal achievement of his *The Five Quintets*, Micheal O'Siadhail now "re-reaps delight, bearing sheaves" in *Testament*, a new harvest of poems. Its two-part sequence, PSALTER and GOSPEL, awakens us to the fresh possibilities of God's reviving presence in our lives. Out of the despair and suffering in his life, the poet memorably sings "a whole choreography of praise" to the Lord for the gift of continuing life and love in these daring and captivating reckonings with and re-imaginings of scriptural texts from the Psalms and the Gospels'.

—**Richard Rankin Russell**, *Professor of English, Baylor University*

'The distinguished poet Micheal O'Siadhail has given us no less than a spiritual classic in his *Testament*, which will captivate and move readers in many future generations. After a lifetime's writing of poetry, which has garnered numerous awards, he has now—in his own words—given us a magnificent "coming out" about his love for God, and has written openly in the form of psalms about the faith that lies, often hidden, in his work. Like the ancient Hebrew Psalms, he offers us a dizzying range of emotions—praise, joy, regret, perplexity, sorrow, hope—and where there is complaint there is also a confidence about having conversation with the Lord of the Dance whom he has called "Madam Jazz" over many years. Speaking in the first person on behalf of us all, his psalms are rooted in a deep experience of life and a relishing of the natural world; they are expressed in innovative language and compelling images which are intensely lyrical and conceptually satisfying at the same time'.

—**Paul S. Fiddes**, *Professor of Systematic Theology, University of Oxford*

'In *Testament*, the poet-psalmist's "I" voices a deeply personal struggle before God: 150 painful-yet-healing steps, from loss, grief, and protest before a God who is not yet present to the defining push-pull of confession and wonderment, remorse and hallelujah before the God whose love is unveiled and veiled again through the eyes of emergent faith. The personal drama performs a spiritual call: that each "I" that marks the other's absence may, through longer or shorter struggles, release its veil and find this Lover waiting'.

—**Peter Ochs**, *Edgar M. Bronfman Professor of Modern Judaic Studies, University of Virginia*

'This book with 150 poems inspired by the Psalms, and 50 inspired by stories from the Gospels, is Micheal O'Siadhail's dialogue with the transcendent. It is a book that is both analeptic and proleptic in that O'Siadhail looks back at a life well lived, as well as looking forward to love, experience and old age. At its core this is a conversation with God: "Now in my mid-seventies, I dare to be more open." This is achieved through a use of language that shows a poet at the peak of his powers, as he praises, rails, doubts, probes but ultimately basks, in a relationship with God. His complex use of rhyme, rhythm, assonance and pararhyme bonds the lines together, and makes the couplets, tercets, quatrains and quinzaines of the poems into remarkably solid, yet fluid, structures. There are hints of John Donne in the *Holy Sonnets* here as God becomes a presence in the lyric dialogue of the poems, while the philosophical influence of T. S. Eliot's *Four Quartets* is here to be seen. It is a valid, fluent and complex testament to the poet's relationship with the divine'.

—**Eugene O'Brien**, *Department of English Language and Literature, Mary Immaculate College*

'This extraordinary book is a spiritual tour de force by one whom I consider to be the greatest living poet writing in English. *Testament* captures in poetry what are for most people of faith the two focal points of Scripture—the Psalms and the Gospels. O'Siadhail has the potential to serve today's church in the way Milton, Bunyan, and Lewis served generations of the faithful in the past. We are blessed to have this work'.

—**Tom Greggs**, FRSE, *Marischal (1616) Chair and Head of Divinity, University of Aberdeen*

'Micheal O'Siadhail stands tall in an illustrious line of Christian poets through the centuries. Conceptually savvy and artistically brilliant, his poetry is breathtaking in its range and beauty. In this new book, O'Siadhail offers a powerful improvisation on classic biblical texts. This book reflects a rich and profound example of a "scriptural imagination" at work. Take and read . . . and savor'.

—**L. Gregory Jones**, *President of Belmont University and Dean and Williams Professor Emeritus, Duke Divinity School*

TESTAMENT

TESTAMENT

Micheal O'Siadhail

BAYLOR UNIVERSITY PRESS

© 2022 by Micheal O'Siadhail

All Rights Reserved. No part of this publication may be reproduced, stored in a retrieval system, or transmitted, in any form or by any means, electronic, mechanical, photocopying, recording, or otherwise, without the prior permission in writing of Baylor University Press.

Cover and book design by Kasey McBeath

Cover art: Delaunay, Robert (1885–1941), Rythme, c.1932 (gouache, w/c & brush & ink on Japon nacré paper), photo © Christie's Images / Bridgeman Images

The Library of Congress has cataloged this book under ISBN 978-1-4813-1628-6.

Library of Congress Control Number: 2022938583

FOREWORD

Now in my mid-seventies, I dare to be more open. Though from the first belief suffused my poetry, when younger I was reticent about naming it. I think I was afraid to be labelled and that my poems might be read through a lens of secular prejudice. In more recent work my angle of vision has been overt. Now I feel a deeper need to give testimony to a source that has sustained my life. *Testament* has two parts: the first I call Psalter, the second Gospel.

Often through my life, when I was exhausted I returned to Norway where I had been a student as a young man. I stayed with old student friends and that usually included at least a week with a couple, Vigdis and Erik Bjørhovde, who lived just outside a town called Raufoss in Eastern Norway. I walked every day about a mile to the top of a nearby hill from where on a clear day you could see far in the distance the great Jotunheim mountain range. On the top of the hill a pious aunt of a friend had raised a stone by the side of the road on which she had engraved the first four lines of Psalm 121: *Jeg løfter mine øyne til fjellene*. . . . There were times when I threw myself on my knees on snow-covered ground and prayed those four lines from the depths of my being:

> I lift my eyes to the mountains—
> > Where does my help come from?
> My help comes from the Lord,
> > The maker of heaven and earth.

This is the cry of the psalmist and I have risked calling this first sequence PSALTER. I love how psalms talk to God in praise and joy, in complaint and grief. No matter how they grumble, they do not doubt their God is there.

Some years ago I worked with the composer and arranger Rob Mathes on a song cycle called *At Night a Song Is with Me* where I wrote responses to extracts from psalms we chose. I remember as I thought deeply about them I became conscious that I so often have had such inner conversations. I began to imagine how I might explore this and see if they might spill out into psalm-like poems. Yet I intended them to be more about God than about me and I trust that the 'I', the first person pronoun, may be broad enough to stand also for the reader. While these conversations are in a modern idiom and do not have the same measure of lamentation or imprecation, I hope, with interwoven and recurring themes, they resonate at least in some fashion with the extraordinary poetry of the original psalms which are still so fresh across millennia.

GOSPEL is a shorter sequence. Here I mediate on stories taken from the New Testament. Most of the episodes I have chosen I have probably known since childhood, yet in some strange way, with one or two exceptions, I don't think I had appropriated them. I was always fascinated by the Marriage

Feast of Cana. I loved the generosity of that first miracle done at the request of a mother. Yet recently as I read a new book on John's Gospel by my closest friend the theologian David Ford, I realised much more fully its symbolism and the whole tone of abundance and overflow which this miracle of turning water into wine signals.

But apart from deepening my own appreciation of these Biblical events, why am I retelling them in poems? Perhaps, as my wife Christina suggested to me, in a similar mode to Leonardo da Vinci painting The Annunciation or Paulo Venese painting The Marriage Feast at Cana, it is an attempt to reawaken the excitement of these episodes. This in turn means urging readers to return to the original telling.

In the case of both PSALTER and GOSPEL praise is the dominant tone. It may be that theologian Walter Brueggemann is right when he suggests that '. . . praise is at the same time and inevitably *a polemical act*'. By this he means, as interpreted by another theologian, Ellen Davis, that the praise of God denies the legitimacy and ultimacy of '"isms" of all kinds that want our loyalty and chase after our life commitment'; these include 'consumerism, militarism, ageism, racism, sexism, and capitalism'. On the other hand I think of these poems less as a polemical act and more as an invitation to return to texts, which Ellen Davis describes so poignantly as 'a lifeline between us and God'.

As a deer longs for flowing streams,
    so my soul longs for you, O God.
My soul thirsts for God,
    for the living God.

—Psalm 42:1–2

St. John tells how, at Cana's wedding feast
The water-pots poured wine in such amount
That by his sober count
There were a hundred gallons at the least.
It made no sense unless to show
Whatsoever love elects to bless
Brims to a sweet excess
That can without depletion overflow.

—Richard Wilbur, from *Wedding Feast*

PSALTER

1

My time ripens, my days mellow.
The lauding cello of this being
I bow, freeing up each string

To praise, to sing, to glorify
The one that I concealed in lines,
In hints and signs, yet out of view

Now plays for you and hums your name.
It wasn't shame that held me back
Or any lack of pride in you—

It's just I knew enough to fear
The Zeitgeist's sneer. Too old to care,
Look how I dare this coming out

And talk about our love out loud.
So hear how proudly I proclaim
My God by name. Uncloseted,

Things once unsaid my life declares:
My words are prayers my being plays;
Through you I gaze at all I love.

2

O impresario of trust,
O maestro of the Bang,
As thirteen billion years ago
You throw desire's half-loaded dice.

How dense your word ballooning out
A span of universe,
Expansive love's intense cocoon
Dilating since the burst began.

Your cloud of elements converge
Appeased by gravity;
From dust's own dark ingredients
You gather stars in galaxies.

See how the world you've slung now spins
To loop its yearly sun;
And how our own frail life begins,
The carbon in primordial soup.

Was this a dice's randomness
Or love's known probabilities
That in your image would make man
To whom you'll send back Noah's dove?

O impresario of trust,
You see me seeing you,
And steward of your love you know
I trust you as you've trusted me.

3

Each richer day in you I bask and breathe
I fill again with gratitude and ask:

How come that I have loved and been so loved,
That you, whose face no one alive has seen,

Allow me glimpse you in each face I know,
When in love's sudden glow you shine,

That you who called from in the burning bush
Speak now to me in cries of all who yearn?

O sweetest God of Abraham and mine,
How can I thank enough that I still am?

So long these bones dwell in my sheath of flesh,
Here in your presence I still bask and breathe.

4

Over seven decades played by ear,
Eleven and three score extempore,
Unplanned, something always sight unseen,
A strumming improvised from riff to riff,
Surprised again by you my Madam Jazz.

When on the fly sometimes I think I sought
To try and call the tune and tie it down,
Forestall how you would stretch me even more.
I knew, or thought I knew, your music's drift
And fought against your syncopated beat.

But you amaze me in my wilfulness,
Erase the bar line I was sure you fixed;
You are the great astonisher, the keen
Creator of surprise ambushing me
With love that dares its sweet and dangerous jazz.

5

I wept salt tears I'd never wept before
Pouring out my flood of grief—
O thief of life should I have raged at you
Who bereaved me of my love?

Should I have groaned and cursed your hallowed name,
Blaming you, my falsest friend,
Who'd end such years by leaving me alone,
Loaning me a love you'd rob?

Was there a calm I should have tried to fake,
Take it on a Stoic chin
And in dumb anger turn a blinder eye,
Trying to deny you, God?

How could you be, in light of what you'd done,
One I could believe in?
But even my denial would avow
How in rage I'd still be yours.

For fear of loss would I have lost it all,
Stalling dark with dark retaliate,
Ungrateful for your given time and so
Throw those years back in your face?

I wept salt tears I'd never wept before,
Wore my heart-grief on my sleeve,
Yet thieving hope from love I'd had,
Glad that such a gift had once been mine.

6

Who dwells in dust for your sake,
Awake and sing! Be delighted!

You blighted hope, broke me down,
Revoking joy, brought love to dust.

You fought me off, turned away—
I yearned for you, hidden God.

Unbidden love you reveal
Renewing me by surprise.

My cries you hear from on high—
How I can love you explore.

You core me out, daring God,
Prepare in me second love's

Unreckoned depths, hew in me
What you again fill with hope.

The thrill of love honed by loss
Atoned for all undergone.

My wonderful late life bliss
Relate a psalm's glowing trust:

He going out weeps and sows—
Re-reaps delight, bearing sheaves.

7

I turn the tap to hot to gush
And douse my now awakened head,
Allow deep time while I unknot
The hitches sleep has tied in me.

The knob on cold, the shower's fresh
Shrill water's thrill will throb my veins;
I thank you that I'm upright still,
My soul returns my flowing cup.

I should first pray and not just wait,
Have said, how grateful, God, I am,
When sleep first let me stir in bed,
My wake-up bleep announcing praise.

But I was snug and tangle-legged,
And in the hug of love's warm bed,
Where two akin become as one.
How could I there have thought of you?

Still in the arms in which I slept,
I thankfully accept your grace;
The wondrous waking I embrace—
Incarnate God you understand.

8

I cry for all who left too soon
I weep for those who had to die—
And you the one who stretched the sky,
I ask you why your canopy
And weather eye protected me,
When some were stranded high and dry?
You mystify me, God. How come
You passed me by when taking them.
And so I wait on your reply
As again I ask you why?

O don't ignore my question, please—
I adore you, God, but even so,
I implore you tell me why
All those with hopes they still lived for,
All those with dreamscapes to explore,
All those who had much more to give,
All those who still had years to soar,
All those who died before they bloomed,
All those too young for death's swing door,
All had to leave the earth's clay floor?

My God, I sigh although I praise,
I groan and magnify at once.
I tie such bonds with loving friends,
Yet one by one they say goodbye.
I shy away from blaming you—
Your business not mine to pry—
Unless you try through them to show,
To teach me how I best should die.
They deserved more life than I,
But you not I stretched out the sky.

9

The sun's glittering corridor bisects
The East River's glinting runs and flows;
A whole morning shivers in its dance

To catch rhythms of your galaxies.
Above all the blur of motion pleases you,
The go-go dance of life, the ocean's stir.

And all things I touch keep dancing too,
The cancans of all the subatomic world,
The hip-hop dance hall of our universe.

We step out between the clay and sky
And take part in every sway and swing
To play in between the quarks and stars.

Across this entire ballroom floor
A whole choreography of praise,
This day's dance a cosmic dance for you.

10

Sleepless nights when guilt can niggle me,
Shame's nervous finger jiggles back and forth,
Racking me with much so long absolved.

Mostly hurt and things I wish undone,
Anguish caused when I was not alert—
I revert and want to try again.

Why do scruples leave no wriggle room,
And dark misgiving still assume my guilt,
Dooming me so I relive each fall?

On my own I try redeeming all,
Want by will alone to wipe slates clean,
Play each flawless scene in retrospect.

Long ago you had forgiven me,
Pardoned all, but please God show me now,
Teach me how I should forgive myself

And allow your love now flow so cleanly through,
Letting me let go and dare trust's deeps.
Grant me, God, your sleep's sweet amnesty.

11

But how should I envisage you?
How do I foresee you God at all?

All-knowing father? Mother earth?
I'd rather have both. No threat

A begetter who hands a language on,
While saying 'I understand although

'All slowly keeps changing over time
By shifts in the range of sound and word.

'You're bound to begin with shape and rule,
So you, my child, first ape, then hone.

'As cloning's no fun, I set you free,
Creating with me what isn't yet'

Begetter, I'm your clerk and aid,
Abettor in love's unending work.

12

My past shines through my present now,
And nothing I have done I disavow,
For in the last analysis,
Both are the music of what is.

Diminished seventh chords' suspense
Holds the present and past tense;
Depending on the key I might
Now cry for sorrow, now delight.

The deepest grief that all grief ends—
For pasts the present makes amends,
As joy again with grief conspires
To wake again untold desires

For both what's glad and sad in song,
Eternities for which I long,
The way tonalities that roam
In slouching semitones turn home

Where they began and still belong,
Where any other end is wrong.
I long for all desires renew,
All yearning, God, now yearns for you.

13

Why am I woken from the womb of night,
A hindsight fight or flight within my brain,
Still urging me to right what can't now change?

No matter how I turn or twist what's done,
Rerun the show, rephrasing this or that
So I'm the one who'd won out in the end,

Although I play my inner video,
Recasting all so I had starred instead
Of fumbling lines, a bumbler caught off guard,

I can't rehearse the way the scene occurred—
Though in my hurt I keep rehearsing how
Next time will be, keep nursing self-regard,

Afraid that I might be perceived as weak.
Of course, it's best to speak against a wrong—
But in my anguish do I seek revenge?

What fragile sense of self has woken me
Or broken ego dream of win or loss,
Provoking me to measure self-esteem?

No need to stand on my own dignity,
What's out of hand I'm handing over now—
All-seeing One, all this you understand.

By night my brain's caprice can master me—
Release me from vainglory's beat-about.
O God of peace, rein in my mind with sleep.

14

I wrestle with the winter night and wake.
The nameless angel's fight now fought and won,
I raise the startled blinds to dazzling light.

The trees that stretch their morning limbs in prayer
All through the breezeless night sang noiseless hymns,
Embraced the whims of snow a freeze has sent.

The sun is sparkling praise in every flake
As one by one they make their hexagon—
But none the same each stakes its claim

To hallow how you love the scattered light,
Allow each flake's own brightness shine,
Each crystal bough a wonder in your sight.

I hear night's angel calling me by name
And in the snow-lit tree do you appear?
You are here a moment then you flee.

Still everything on which I lay my eye
Desires to praise and glorify your name.
I like Jacob see your face and live.

15

God, did you then break my heart
So for your sake I'd kiss the rod of grief,
And let you make me trust your love's abyss?

When you hid your face from me,
I shunned despair's embrace although I sorrowed,
I let the dawn outpace night's borrowed dark.

Only what you willed my prayer:
Whatever, where or what or who or why.
In your care I left what's left for me,

Banking on how chance is yours,
No notice in advance and warningless
You turned my hunchback mourning into dance.

Should I now be dismayed at how,
Though grateful still, my memories will fade
And time will trade what is for all that was?

I'm so here and now again.
You fill my cup once more with sheer delight,
And every year I've left my year of hope.

Dance you say and dance I will;
I trust my thanks and kiss what's gone goodbye.
Let all that was still safely lie with you.

16

Seeing friends some dozen years ahead
Sunken-cheeked and frail once pioneers,
Heroes, shrunken blazers of a trail,
Pale stars, their peers now mostly dead,
All of who I am reveres them still.

Maybe I should dread to be that way,
Fear the day I start to fail? And look!
How my jet head is greying now so fast.
Don't abandon me I pray you, God,
Don't forsake me when life drains away.

Drivenness is past, all zeal and aim,
Goals, pursuit of fame, the jockeying,
Playing roles, all striving for success.
Bless my milder salt and pepper years,
Give me love's largesse as I grow old.

In the end what other aim would count?
I've no other final dividend
Only praise I give, the friend embraced.
Grant me my career's remaining dream:
Years to leave love's legacy behind.

17

Tell me I can't conceive what you've in store,
Even imagine your paradise,
Sunlit walled garden Eve recalls in us.

Tell me how every last breath will take to flight,
Glorious bird crying farewell,
Love from its shell transferred to paradise.

Tell when that dark will fall we home,
Though we all eat from the apple tree,
Sweating our brow on heaven's long haul.

Who could be harsh enough to fill our hearts,
Cruel enough to so instil
Longing that still persists as we go?

Who could have brimmed my mind with vain desires,
Need to explain, such need to find
Meaning behind our mundane quick come and go?

God, it's to you my longing will return.
Give me sweet life till I adjourn—
Exile from Eden my yearning dwells in you.

18

Did you wait out some thirteen billion years
For one hundred billion galaxies
Before this sundered globe might now be one?

Or those three hundred thousand years or more
Since we blundered out of paradise
I wonder if you wondered how or when

We upright bipeds fumbling centuries
Might just tumble to what's cyber space,
Stumble on how this wide world is one?

Did you all-knowing know this in advance,
See beforehand how we'd chance on skills—
Or take a lover's stance allowing time?

Yet even lovers surely celebrate,
After waiting eons for a dream,
However late. Now brother's keepers all

Though slow to learn, Cain's children bear your sign—
No excuse will do—your world now one.
When you enquire where Abel is we know.

19

If noiseless,
Would I have groped the dark
And moped from day to day,
Embraced despair?

I can't imagine life without these words,
These sounds to soothe each inner strife, console
A heart so rife with rainbow moods.

If choiceless,
How could I then have coped
Or hoped all would be well,
Or that you care?

I can't imagine meaning in my days
Without a phrase, an utterance to vent
My praise and thank you that I've seen the sun.

If voiceless . . .
But words evoked a trust
And cloaked me in your love.
My life's a prayer.

20

The stymied dawn can't redden where it should,
A leaden morning's sky and river merge.
Though dry, will greyness deaden all my day?

Now even sky and concrete walls converge
To leave me in a mood where wonder palls.
My whole life stalls. My God, can I believe in you,

Believe beyond the dullness that now falls,
A numb despondency of this nor that,
The flatness of all things when you abscond?

No gloss or shine—the finish is all matt;
I dread this loss, all sign of lustre gone,
Across the spectrum hues of joy resign.

But wait! This morning is just Babylon—
I'll trust in exile my blind date with you,
I must not yet anticipate the day.

The only trust is trusting through and through,
In love to trust halfway won't do I know,
And while nonplussed by gloom I'm true and fast.

Though understanding dread, please sun me now;
Incarnate and unplanned instead caress
This flesh and touch with love's red blooded hand.

21

Bless these arms I wrap around in love,
These caressing hands of clay,
Fondling nonetheless eternal hope.

Hallow this mouth of mine that savours sound,
Lips that kiss and pine for more,
Tongue that tips and swishes passion's sign.

Mark my eyes that gaze at other eyes
Endlessly amazing me,
Though I praise, my praise falls always short.

Set apart these ears to hear love's words
Saying all I take to heart,
As sweet nothings spoken chart delight.

Favour this nose with sheets' fresh redolence,
Pillows' dents of fragrant sleep,
Liquid soap and watered scents of skin.

Though the Vikings crave Valhalla's heat,
Further south breezes blow
Cooling paradise's glowing sun;

Others dream of feasting, wine and song,
Timeless floating on cloud nine—
Heaven is still mine both here and now.

Jazz Madam if you allow me pass
Judgement day's exam, then please
Re-embody me just as I am,

Fold me in this carnal envelope,
Hold as one this flesh and soul.
Truth be told, I want to be this me.

But too much I'm in and of the world—
Let me rise above my clay.
Pardon me how much I love this earth.

Heaven knows what we are waiting for,
What you've in store I can't now know.
Adoring you, I bow my head and pray.

22

Did every war evoke your name,
Claiming you were on each side,

Deciding your intent for sure,
All presuming your consent?

Relentlessly still seeking you,
How to know where you will speak?

So weak your voice in outcast cries,
Crying out 'Are you that friend

'Who in the end will care for me?
Do you love me? Dare I love?'

23

Open the door, let me into the room,
Into the inner room of my mind,
Into where I begin to unwind,
Into a chamber of riotous prayer.

Though it had begun overcast,
Morning sun has burnt through the cloud;
One to one I'm praising out loud,
Babbling amazement and gratitude.

How could anyone now sing dumb?
Somehow nothing has happened I feel,
Nothing mine and nothing for real,
Till I seal it with outbursts of thanks.

Though my debt to you has no end,
Listening to your silence I let
This half-audible sweet duet
Fill my room until it expands,

Finds a place for endless high hopes
Thanks in mirror image still sees —
Overture and a reprise,
Full of your eternal desire.

What I ask I allow you decide.
How can life have happened to me?
What I thank for who'd dare to foresee?
Is all prayer a space for surprise?

24

What was the quest or what was the desire?
Was I obsessed with fame?
To what did I aspire? To be the best?

You must have understood that early need,
To just succeed, to make a mark;
Our youth demands to supersede the past.

You must too know how in our middle years,
Ambition fears all compromise,
Serenity implies careers have failed.

Such peace admitting I no longer care —
Enough that I have done my bit.
Whatever gifts that you saw fit to give,

Whatever genes that loved the sound of words
That found their way to me
Redound now to the glory of your name.

And freer than I have ever been before,
I pour my drunken words of praise,
Adore you for the sake of who you are.

25

O noiseless lover, can I be sure you hear?
Can I rely on you
To see everything that I do and think,
My swings of mood?
Does nothing elude your omniscience?

Unnerved by silence how can I be sure you know
My story blow by blow,
Each cameo of my full biography?
Can you keep count
So all-knowingly of this amount of me?

What of every lone soul existing through
The whole of time—
Could you control such an information flow,
Not find too much
To register and to keep all in mind?

But how I underrate such capaciousness.
With you who'd create
A universe how could we come to grips?
Our chips and bytes
Seem flickers in your scorching sunlight's gaze.

Your muteness rooms so much more than speech.
I must watch for
Your semaphore that transmits your tacit thoughts
And inner signs.
In sunlit trust, I must soak your silence in.

26

Help me now! I feel the skew of hate.
Show me how to deal with loathing eyes,
Blind to who I know I really am.

I can prove it isn't true at all.
Can't they see me as I do? Oh no!
There's no reason in a jaundiced view.

Should I call on you to show your wrath,
Let the haters know just what is what?
In the end I'll have to let it go.

Why react to hate with greater hate?
Then the fact is we would bond in rage —
Magnets that repel also attract.

Still I'm only human and I'm frail;
I can fill with anger and self-doubt,
Grill myself and ask if it's all true:

Has my life the meaning they construe?
Hate could skew my image of myself —
Tell me you remember who I am.

27

How come such fearfulness in me?
Such angst could numb my spirit's leap
And keep my life from taking flight.

Then why this fear of losing face,
All bets still hedged for fear of loss,
Disgrace eschewed at any cost?

How often dread of failure too
Could make me tread too cautiously,
Instead of daring come what may.

Afraid of lack or poverty
Did fright once have me on the rack,
Hold me back from lavishness?

Or panics at the thought of death,
Dark moments fraught with fear
Prevent me dancing as I ought?

Too scared to lose a lifetime's love,
Has doubt impaired advice I gave,
Withholding what I should have shared?

How slowly, slowly year by year,
I know you hear and set me free.
My heart is steadfast, I will not fear.

28

Why have you turned your face away from me?
Is this the bleakest day of all my life?

The cloth of love in which you wrapped my heart
You've torn apart. I don't know where to turn.

In my confusion, I slither near despair.
O hear me out even if you will not look!

I cry to you and beg you on my knees
Not to abandon me. On you I still rely.

If I've failed, no bridges left to burn,
And all my flags are nailed now to your mast.

You act as if you do not care and yet
I can't deny you in my near despair.

My God, my God, please return to me.

29

Rainbow birds, flamingo and blue jay,
Rusted chaffinch on its white barred wing;
Panoplies of hues delight in you.

Shimmered pinks of ling below the sea,
In dark ponds carp's glimmered scales;
Every glimpse unveils your majesty.

Spotted orchids praying in a marsh,
Common twayblades broad paired leaves,
Countless breeds applaud all you create.

Painted ladies and red admirals,
Spanned eyespots on peacock butterflies
Spread their wings to flutter accolades.

In each display of hues and spots and stripes,
Beauty both attracts and frightens prey,
Purpose mixed with play keeps praising you.

30

With mother's milk the hushaby
All will be well no need to cry —
O promise me she didn't lie.

Although we know of death's goodbye,
We swear a love that will not die —
O promise me that we don't lie.

Eternities of joy deny
Time's ruthless arrow on the fly —
O promise that they do not lie.

We laugh and laughing you're nearby,
All fun is reaching for your sky —
O promise that it doesn't lie.

Here under your eternal eye,
I want to trust your lullaby —
O promise that you do not lie.

31

When I subvert your caring plans for me,
I wonder, God, are you a lover hurt
Less by what foolish things I dare to do,
More how I'm not aware of wounding you?

And do you know the ache of hidden wounds
Still hoping for unbidden words to show
At least I know how I have anguished you
And how I'm flying in the face of love?

Or do you feel a lover's inward shame
Because you have to name the hurt and so
You undergo things done and thoughtlessness,
The double blow of pain inflicted twice?

Oh yes! Yet you're the lover who can wait
Eons to create by chance and choice
A dance of molecules that start the cells
From which evolve each life you take to heart.

I slowly realise how I transgress
And you who saw me fall will watch me rise;
No need to fret. You've all the world of time
And yet you still desire my wounding love.

32

God, you know this ache to leave a trace,
Need to scratch, somehow make our mark —
Catching what no one ever can.

Words we choose trying hard to snatch
Moods that shift, matching then with now —
We crave both fixity and drift.

Overtones climbing sweet desire
Drop in time tearful semitones —
Music yearns both for here and there.

Paint holds on, canvassing delight,
Moments gone longing clones in oil —
Wistfulness both bemoans and fetes.

Every sound, pitch and smear of clay
Fearing loss, claims a holding place,
Space for where we can long for you.

33

Each year I live the richer years become —
I feel the nearness now of all the earth,
This clay where I belong from birth to fall.

Every season courses through my blood —
The sap that wakes from winter's reverie,
Each bud that breaks, each tumbling crimson leaf.

Such bursts of yellows, reds and blues,
Vibrating hues of light that flood my veins
Ignite a spectrum of your glory's praise.

As though when ebbing life accelerates,
You show so much that must have passed me by,
Holding back what's most intense till last.

Aware how my genetic tape runs down,
I risk this bliss I didn't dare before —
Could paradise be half as good as this?

This earth's splendour I can hardly bear —
My bore must be too slender still for you.
Are you preparing me for more and more?

34

How has it all happened as it has,
How in the jazz of things
Did every callow dream I dreamt
Become this life I now enjoy?

How can it be so that this is true,
That all should go to plan,
That every wish should ride its horse,
Youth's reverie become my life?

But, God, I did not have a plan as such —
No plot, no grand design,
More something that I knew I had to do,
As if it's you kept driving me.

Yet you do not drive, you only let
Desire's lone driving gene
Endeavour to catch in rhythm's words
Inklings of forever love.

What else could a passionate nature do
When nothing else but you
Allays a strange forlornness deep in me —
Desire had dazed me from the start.

Although it all happened as it has,
Much as my callow dream,
Through all that's unforeseen where dreams come true
Desire for you my steering gene.

35

Sometimes, God, you confuse me so—
Though I want what is best for all,
How to know if I have chosen well?

Why do I always suffer to grow?
Why are you trying me once again,
On the ground here beneath your sky?

Can't I grow just by rising above
All the mess, all distress below,
Ripen in your resplendent glow?

Here I am caught in the daily flow,
Dramas I can never ever predict
Or programme, always guessing the plot.

Give me clues I'm still struggling for,
Just some cues, prompts where I miss my line.
Please, I beg, don't confuse me so.

36

It has dawned again on all you move,
You have drawn the curtains from your skies.

As in paradise so too on earth,
Insurgent love as you entice the sun

Now to silver our East River's flow;
All creation's on the go once more.

You speak and seem to beckon from beyond —
I respond. A story re-begins.

Contradicting voices, judgements past,
Choices taken, vexed decisions made.

Every option shapes my storyline,
You, by design, involve me in —

Past unfolding towards a future tense
Making sense of where I am for now.

How can I keep pace with you, my God?
Witness I embrace this day with you

Yielding to the mystery of plot,
History you knit before my eyes.

37

You are a great interrupting God!
When things are set you create a stir,
As if you do not understand
How all's planned and safe,
As you enthral me with intense desire.

I long to know clearly where I stand,
But when I think all is now just so,
And everything straightened out —
No need to hesitate —
Some fresh and wild upsurge desiring you.

You cross the boundaries of flag and clan,
Your open plan keeps dreaming up new goals;
Unseaming all that I have sewn
You bend my comfort zone
Allowing me no clear end in sight.

My need to tame you will soon expose
And all I close you will open up.
No objective and no aim,
No framework will now do,
Beyond how I must still yearn for you —

My journey here one journey of desire.

38

Should I now find another name for you?
Often we've sought to tame and own you, though
You get the blame for all done in your name.

Over again I try to nail you down
Capturing you to fit my scale of thought,
Failing to magnify your name and word.

Easy look back and seek a mythic past,
Perfect epoch that time has undermined,
Golden domain where you're confined and owned.

Come and seduce me, I'm besotted with you,
Ravish me again and juice my straight-laced soul —
Loose in your glory I will spill your praise.

Tired of what's shallow and cramped, I refuse
Fallow gold pasts, as shamelessly, God, I
Hallow your name in love's eternal now.

39

How do I speak of this unseeable one?
Will I say he when I do not say you,
Even if he's neither sex or both?

How should I dare describe this God of mine,
Maybe a hidden face that's everywhere,
All the more caring as the absent one,

Searched but absconded countenance that shines,
Bond of love here speaking deep within
Whispering sacred rumours of beyond

Keeps on reminding me how small I am
In the sweep of quasars' lavish time,
Faintest bleep on heaven's monitor.

Now I'm aware how frail it all can be,
Ready to kneel and dare be smitten by him,
Summoning up a presence I know will care.

So it begins as love affairs begin —
Both admit that each of us now cares.
You desire all my prayers and praise.

40

The God who hid Moses in a rock
And laid his hand blocking up the cleft
Afraid in case Moses see his face,
Still shows us those sacred lineaments,
Disclosing light through his fingers' gaps.

Those times I glimpse glory in a gaze —
A smile's embrace, gesture, glance or laugh —
I seize my chance, sneak previews of God,
And peek ahead, catching his dazzling mien,
I've seen my God's countenance and lived.

Each time I've heard cries of brokenness,
Allowed my sure heart to chime in grief,
I know I've been through the pillared cloud,
I've walked inside, seen the meeting tent —
As friends I've talked face to face with God.

41

Of course, our lives go on no matter how,
All things exist, no call to find their source;
It's come-day go-day whether I do or not.
Guess what! We have no need of any god.

And so, can he be grander than our need,
Beyond necessity — an overflow,
A flare of colour in a silken dress,
The daring of a hat just worn for fun?

Or maybe the abundance of a song
That pours from a heart that's stunned by love,
A line that soars against a counterpart,
A lifetime's longing so condensed in words?

Or where a shapely tool exceeds its use,
A lamp's curved shade, some lovely kitchenware,
A clean-limbed chair, a coupe soup bowl well-made,
A red pine table laid by lavish hosts?

In all this plenitude a splendour hides.
I'm sure my God abides in life's excess.

42

Tell me why are you doing this to me?
Don't you know how I miss all those you take?

One by one you are robbing me of friends
None should lose, as if death's blind hit-and-run

Raids my life and insisting on its share,
Snatches friends to install among the shades.

Yet why them and not me I'll never know.
You allow your creation's flow to work,

Trusting how in the end a love that's free
Can't foresee or command a charted course.

In good faith I will caress rife memories
As I live to the full, match loss with life,

For my sake, will you tell each friend I've loved,
Tell them how I still spend their lives in mine?

43

Forgive me, God, how little I have done.
O no! I didn't shun them or just see
Another bum. I've tried to show I cared
And so I gave some change. Was that enough?
Was it an easy out, my saving face?

Every beggar, every down-and-out,
The stray, the layabout, the destitute
I pass still stare at me as if to say,
You think you see me but I know you don't,
If you did why won't you hear my cry?

I do, I do! I hear that ceaseless cry—
Believe me, please how as I'm passing by
I'm ill at ease because I know I've seen
The drifter I too might so well have been.
I know that through your eyes they stare at me.

Was I too driven, too enamoured of words?
Should I have given you my life through them—
Not just to hear that cry but heed and tend
The broken, spend my spell of given years
To wipe the tears from your all-seeing face?

44

A spring and the leaves are all see-through green,
Another full ring has circled within the bole —
The juice in my soul begins to rise and sing.

I praise an extravagant creator's urge
To burgeon again, to splurge gratuitous sap,
Once more the unbidden surge of fearless growth.

A winter's nude trees had seemed so pained and dark
As if they had given up and hadn't dreamed
Of sap that so often had redeemed their hurt.

A hurt can beget a hurt, more wars, more feuds,
A merry-go-round of settling older scores,
There's such sweet relief when bitter sores can heal.

God's spring has arrived and how could I hold a grudge?
I shed any grievance or old resentment's pain,
Turn over new leaves unfolding deep within.

45

Why can't I find you, God? Where are you now?
My phone has pinged just to remind me how
I have an unread text whose fretful tone
Demands I tend to it—instead I have
An urgent email which I need to send.

I'm so distracted by so many things,
Whole lists of stuff I'm keeping on the go,
No matter how I try, it's not enough—
Whatever space I have I don't know why
I'm checking my new messages in case.

How can I reach you, God, or hear your voice?
Assuage my busyness and teach me how
To still such cravings to engage my mind
And let it float and fill with streams of thought
That drift beyond all things it ought to do.

Let reverie then slowly channel me,
To where my memories and hopes both flow
And by degrees allow the peace and space
For you, my God, to occupy, as in
Such stillness I begin to dwell in you.

46

Nude and weak I left the womb behind —
Past my peak will I grow feeble yet?

God, you frame my life so I depend
From my birth to end on others' aid.

Though a pride pretends to walk alone,
I admit how all my life depends on friends.

I would die in black holes of the self —
I'm only I in light of those I love.

Is dependency your plan in case
I form a carapace to hide within?

In my reliance you are coring me,
Hollowing me out to love you more.

47

No happy-end ridings on into the sun
As violins play,
My God is a god who's beginning again.

All things shall be well, in the long run I trust.
My life clings to this,
However times turn on his grand carousel.

I'm no optimist—in the short term I know
How God can so thwart
What I've desired, my intentions dismissed.

I know bitter wind can both sting and unnerve,
And skinned by the cold
How God, it can seem, has rescinded my spring,

But still I will cling though this God may abscond.
Beyond winter dark,
Beyond the cold wind, in the long run I trust.

Heartbreaker who mends by still waking my hope,
My mover who'll shake,
Fresh-start recreator, my maker of springs.

48

According to plan, I should be old and ripe.
Forgive me, God, a Peter Pan in me

Desires more life to live and savour yet —
I cannot get enough of earthly things,

I know how parents once assuaged their fears:
In spite of years their minds had never aged.

O yes, my mind but please my body too!
My clay has not resigned from its delights.

I still enjoy all pleasures of the flesh,
Each day afresh I look, I touch, I kiss.

More than three score and ten not good enough?
The time of life I should be saying prayers?

I do and ask you, God, to give me more,
To let me live more fully day by day.

Although I'm in, not of this mortal world,
I am, you see, still so in love with life.

49

My God, you wager on choice and so
I know you'll never control or drive.

In all I've done, I took charge myself,
Each pro and con I assessed and weighed.

I stumble on, opting for this or that—
There's much I miss, much I bumble now.

But somehow still when the chips are down
I dodge small slips, and don't make mistakes

That set in train lifetimes' of misery.
I know I'm free, yet there is so much

I sense, so much nobody understands—
As if by stealth some wise hand half-steers,

As if, my God, I can read your hints
And heed soft words I don't know I've heard.

50

Psalmists once too severe condemned
Out of hand all transgressors for fear
They might doubt your repute, my God.

You're not angry each day with me,
You don't curse every time I stray;
Yet what's worse than offending you?

Worse perhaps not to know then how
Your compassion atones each lapse—
I'm so sure this must hurt you more.

Yes, I've fallen, have missed the mark,
Falling short, too much done was wrong—
Still I long for your olive branch.

So I release with a Noah's trust
Dawn's white dove to return with peace.
You still love me, my jilted God.

51

You're the one I take for granted so
Come what may I know you're there for me;
I can go about my day to day,
Confident I have no need to doubt.

I am not a lover starting out,
Always wondering what the other thinks,
Nervous if I've understood the hints,
Whether I have acted as I should.

Yet like any lover you still need
Praise, to know that I will not forget
What an endless gift you promise me.
I depend on you no matter what.

Hand in glove, enchanted we enjoy
Take-for-grantedness of mindful love.

52

Dazzler of minds, my Madam Jazz,
Lover who binds and binding frees,

Time and again I name you God,
One and the same, the one invoked.

Maybe I should sing litanies,
Name upon name, a whole array:

Blessed be He, The Holy One,
Light beyond Light, but nonetheless

Skirting around unutterable you.
So I revert and call you God.

53

You are the midpoint, nub of all,
The hub from where your tethered pen
Has drawn circumferences shared;

Here gathered round your circle's girth
We earthlings hesitate to share
The radiation of your truth.

And though we try to own you, God,
Though diametrically at odds,
Each spoke still meets in your eye.

For you are where we concentrate,
You are the focus of all prayer.
We're each as far as we are near.

54

You have beset me behind and before —
David the psalmist defined your regime.

Even the dark is not darkness to you;
Nothing can hide in the dance-driven quark.

Nowhere not even the blackest of holes
Stores its enigmas unknown to your mind.

Each of my hope's and my memory's log,
All my biography safely archived,

Data that's stowed in your infinite base,
Deep in your graphene's eternal space.

Here in your presence now like it or not —
Either I'm blind or become a seer.

Even before any word's on my tongue,
Surely you know I believe in your love?

55

Madam, I'm walking on air on top of the world,
You see I'm carefree and head over heels in love.

The late evening sun is now singeing the trees,
A breeze is blowing soft kisses extolling you.

Your glory sings out among passers-by —
So let the world and who lives here shout for joy!

Even the honk of commuting cars acclaim
Your splendour and exalt your name tonight.

The bricks and girders of buildings bend to you,
Their fire escapes all ascend like Jacob rungs

To seventh heaven, where you see I'm over the moon,
Where all creation in tune is praising you.

56

Among the swirling crowd
Again I pray out loud,
A delinquent chanting his nones;
And so proud

To bless each passer-by,
All hallowed on the fly,
To let my prayers be high-flown drones
Sent to spy

On what you hold in store,
Desires I have and more,
You, giver of great unknowns
Unlooked for

In your unbalanced finance—
Your grace a cash advance,
Our lives are always payday loans.
In my trance

Creation comes on strong
In brazen-mouthed song
Picks up my sky-high overtones,
Plays along,

Forecasting heaven's days.
I stroll this bustling maze
The music of being in my bones.
And I praise.

57

Why start to carp as we begin to age—
What an almighty mess your world is in?

Never allow me, God, to turn back clocks
Let me still yearn for all that's yet to come.

Happy to feed with praise as I was fed,
Let me so bless as many once blessed me.

Youth will renew what we must now bequeath,
Rumours of you among your heirs to love.

Given new hunger for truth I know we leave
Trusting to younger dreams to mend your world.

58

Imagination's God you're launching me
To steer by stars and signs I can't yet see.

Deep down I know I want things as they are—
And letting be is surely best by far.

But is the price of growth this risk of pain—
Must I dream again against the grain?

But staying still I know I drift behind,
I'll stall unless my course is redesigned.

O God of your creation's non-stop change
Why do you stretch me now beyond my range?

Inviting me to be myself and more
You dare me grow as I have grown before.

59

Memory's own desires seem to search its database—
Every face I have known now returns to shine on me.

No one loved is effaced from my scrolling down screen.
Why wipe out or delete? All are mine who once I embraced.

Yes, so many are gone where they're hidden away by you.
Even still I hold on to each countenance and name.

I'm recalling these lives so inscribed and deep in me—
Though alone as I trawl I re-summon a closeness lost.

Moved apart or just drifting away and out of sight—
Some I might have re-found but I didn't make the time.

Seeing now how my desires to hold on are limitless,
Hold me, God, in your cradle of meshed nanowires

So sustained by your being's own worldwide web,
I will trust in the linkage of your all-seeing love.

60

Forgive me how I must repeat myself—
Every day I live
I say my prayer of thanks.

Today again my heart will overflow
And then as yesterday
Once more I say amen

To every psalm of gratitude I know
And so each day renewed
Obey my overflow

And try to find another way to thank
As I reiterate
How I appreciate

The way you've lavished love on me.
You see psalms parallel,
Impel you now to hear

The swell of joy in me that's crying out
To know how can it be
I'm so in love I must

As any lover does repeat myself,
So many times declare:
My God, I give you thanks.

61

Maybe I cannot see your face and live—
You must remain a faithful absentee,
Present in traces, in a hint or clue.

Though you allow me such free will to choose,
Still I presume your watchful twinkling eye,
Smiling by times that I have been surprised,

Stunned by the way you ignore what I sought,
How you pre-empt the needs I thought were mine,
Giving me more than I had dreamt I'd have.

Did I just catch a glance? But you abscond.
On my behalf you dream beyond my need.
Though I can't see you, I'm sure I hear your laugh.

62

So much we've done to smooth our sojourn here
Turning 'round one sun that counts each year.

Is doubt a treason, another Eden's fall?
Reason trusts itself to master all.

We cure, we thrive, we fly, we walk the moon,
Make this world keep dancing to our tune.

And yet caretakers of your world transgress,
Overstep our bounds in our excess.

The icebergs melt, the summer swelters surge—
Is there still time to pull back from the verge?

Whatever we can do can't be too soon—
We who overreach now change our tune.

Forgive us sojourners who've lost the grip—
Teach us, God, again our stewardship.

63

The wind is gathered in your fist
And in your garments waters bound—
I've been in irons, run aground.

I've waited till my bow fell off,
My tiller centered, sail trimmed in,
I've close-hauled without chagrin.

Headway, sternway or sideways,
All points I need to sail I learn,
I beat and reach and run in turn.

My head to wind I've heaved to—
The gale too much when I had tacked—
Then helm to weather, foresail backed.

I compromise, so full and by,
Though sidewise more, my course less true,
I am still beating home to you.

64

No, how could I know when broken down?
Heartsick who'd have understood
How I fall apart
To allow me recompose myself?

Did your world evolve from such unrest,
Newer order first expressed
In fragile lapped seams that burst,
Freeing dreams that then re-organise

In their hidden woven ways
Such unbidden living things.
Still life clings to what it knows—
No one ever chose the aches of growth.

After all such chaos threatens us—
It might prove too much for us to take.
For my sake you push me to the edge.
In my breaking down you build me up.

65

Madam Jazz, what do I know of your time,
Counting out the years you intend to allot?

You're the drumbeater whose lead hand I hear,
You're the high hat whose fixed rhythm I still heed.

You're the pacemaker, the throb I tap to,
Rapping closed cymbals to match my heart's beat.

Yes, the back beat you catch on your snare—
Startle me, catch the first beat on your crash,

Shock me with kickdrums that can pound out the pulse,
Play a fill knocking two beats on the toms.

You surprise, thrill me above and beyond—
Still the firm beat of your love's metronome.

66

The earth is the Lord's, the fullness thereof—
But, Lord, you still trust us from above

To treasure this habitat we loan,
To cherish what we can never own;

As tenants at will we're passing through,
Where all that we hold belongs to you.

How finely you've interwoven all,
All balanced so in your longer haul

Unless unawares we interfere,
All flourishes in your biosphere.

O teach us to steward what self-sustains,
To count what's lost in wanton gains!

Sojourning between each forbear and heir,
Show us your caretakers how to care.

67

The morning's heavy sky is closed and fraught
With snow that won't allow the dawn to flush
A gloom that in my youth I'd often fought.

Almighty, I've no knock-down proof of you—
You're far beyond the reach of any thought,
All logic fails, no argument will do,

No image can contain you, no similitude.
Beyond our being, words now falter too—
Superlatives compare, infinitude

Here stands apart from all we can define
And every name I give you still elude;
No matter how I try you hold the line.

I know no one can see your face and live,
Allow me hear your voice, give me a sign!
Although you're never argumentative

Whatever you desire you will disclose
In words; insisting on the figurative,
You're poet-God who will not speak in prose

But sends allusive lines from high-command
With metaphors refusing to foreclose
The mystery of how you show your hand.

But now the sun has dared a kindled blush—
I listen for your voice as here I stand
Unsandalled still before your burning bush.

68

Mysterious unseen beyond my scope
So every utterance falls short of you—

My hidden one who listens out of view
You fill me with such longings and strange hope.

What is it in your silence I can hear
So far above my earthling ken and reach—

And yet I name you in my mundane speech.
How are you both so other and so near?

But hidden you have chosen to inspire
My praise. Who can grasp your majesty?

Invisible yet radiant in me
You commandeer my yearning and desire.

69

O One who both can bless and count my days
O light from light, with all I am I praise.

Relentless life, though bodied, undefined—
Your signature in energies you've signed.

Your stones cry out, the panting deer still yearns.
O pillar of cloud, O speaking bush that burns,

You waited out all time to call my name.
Like Moses I now hide my face in shame

Before your power that hoists the morning star.
Almighty who before all is you are.

70

Silently you overwhelm me, God!
Why have I become your lightning rod?

Those who hate me wait now in delight—
Job and Jeremiah both were right.

Prisoner of hope you test so far,
Yet I love you still for who you are.

Bearing me your grieving Ichabod,
Dark and humble mystery of God

You're still silent as the satin night.
Dreaming up returns still out of sight,

Exile in your blindly homing maze,
Even in my grief I still will praise.

71

All powerful, you whom I adore,
Should your will alone be done,
Should you be the cause of all,

Then, is even Adam's fall
Nothing in the longer run—
What we will you just ignore?

Neither bully nor the cause,
Gently you, my God, invite
Me to fathom such desire

You engender and inspire.
Generous in all your might,
You allure by love not laws,

As your humble glory rings
Out, attracting from above,
Willing to entice and win

By such power you've hidden in
Signs and fragrance of a love,
Cradled in a world of things.

72

Begging all I think I need,
Not my will but yours be done,
I your creature still concede.

You, though utterly the One
Faithful to your covenant
And creation's longer run

May not grant what I now want,
You are hearing what I say,
Heeding me your supplicant.

In hallowed space, here I obey,
Take my time up into yours,
Bend to where in dust I pray.

Changelessly your will endures,
Yet incarnate in your care,
God, your listening reassures.

Even silent words you share
Endlessly caress my need,
Bless this commerce of love's prayer.

73

But why did you create all this?
A whim, some vagary from afar
That conjured worlds from the abyss—
Or just your being who you are?

You speak your lavish 'let there be'?
For you are light before you hang
The sun and moon or seed a tree,
Or life evolves from love's big bang.

In you what's free and need are one
And you can do just as you will;
As rivers flood and overrun,
Your being has to overspill.

For all your nature's overflow,
You fill or ebb if need should be—
Your power a power you can forego,
As you in your humility

Withdraw again with tact and grace,
Less boss than patron who suggests.
You bless and warm our planet's face,
A host fulfilled by praising guests.

74

Is it endlessness I crave? Why fill
Me with such desires for paradise,
Yearnings for eternity in you.
Tell me why such longings never cease,

Why in longing I alone find peace?
You're eternity that I pursue—
Nothing less than you will now suffice,
In your presence time itself holds still.

You're eternity and do not stand
Outside my world in empty timelessness;
Every moment is inscribed in you.
You enfold our hours in who you are.

Millennia of every unseen star
Beaming forth what's infinite and true.
You in turn illuminate and bless
Holding nanoseconds in your hand,

Your foreverness envelops me.
Even if I have no need to climb
Out of worldly days, I'm overjoyed
By eternal moments you avow.

Let me feel your hidden nearness now,
Breathe your spirit on our aeons' void,
Stoop down in beauty to redeem earth's time—
Take me up in you, eternity.

75

Some have wondered, some have agonised
Whether Madam Jazz knows all before
We have played our notes both sweet and sour.

How we underrate her music's power!
More than notes, the whole abundant score,
Sum of every riff we've improvised,

All of what is never said and done,
Backbeat syncopations on the move,
Jazzed ad-libs covertly homeward bound,

Radiance of each impromptu sound,
Taken up into my Madam's groove
Where to know and be are all the one.

Open to the way we pray and yearn,
Hearing each extemporising heart,
Madam humbly seeming to abscond

Bides within and yet remains beyond,
Both involved and perfectly apart,
Reckons still on my resolved return.

76

For sure God throws a lover's dice
Yet knows each creature's secret mind—
All pettiness and all desires,
Our every virtue, every vice,
And yet this lover never tires.

But should I fear this knowing eye
That sees too much of who I am—
A human carnal to the hilt?
Can this great lover still stand by
And love me in such naked guilt?

What is this shame that often gnaws?
Because I mock a neighbour's faults,
Do I in turn expect the same,
So how I scorn another's lack
Now turns in me into self-blame?

My maker knows my whereabouts
And sees all suffered through my eyes;
No tyrant God or thought-police,
Respecting each mind's ins and outs,
Withdraws to leave my soul in peace.

Whether I fly on morning wings
Or land beyond the sea, well known
My every failure, all my falls.
Although I know who knows all things,
Where are you, Adam? God still calls.

77

As though alone above
In endless open space
God needed me to love,

Desiring my embrace
To warm the empty vasts
And leave a caring trace—

As though all life contrasts
With silent vacancies'
Chill blasts and counterblasts

To give a maker ease,
Who waits on my caress—
As though I would appease

An anxious loneliness!
My God is love that needs
No aim but pours life's yes

Abundantly and feeds
My hungers deep within.
Such lavishness exceeds

In love I can't begin
To match from here below.
What passion is akin

To needless overflow?
My God is not forlorn.
All love I give I owe.

78

Many let no present fit the bill
But instead tenaciously
In their bygones seek rebirth,
Golden age's sacred cow
Treads imagined paths it never trod.

Doctrinaires believe they can at will
Shortcut humanity,
Forcing all for all their worth
For ideas they avow
In some future's name to kiss the rod.

In eternity all time stands still—
What was, what is and what will be;
As in heaven so on earth,
Silent dynamo of now,
Dark and humble mystery of God.

79

How I want to rein my Madam in,
Wish to know where jazzing goes,
Hear the final cadence in advance.

Must Madam always lead me such a dance,
Keep me always on my toes?
Wildly improvising I begin.

All would be so easy to decide—
Only let me comprehend
Where my Madam's unknown dance will lead!

Madam Jazz knows all too well my need
To restrain, but in the end
Nothing in her jazz is cut and dried.

Now the blues and now it's funky soul,
Shifting tempo to surprise,
As her grooves keep switching on the hoof,

Fills and crashes too can raise the roof—
Madam's tunes extemporise.
In her riffing I must cede control.

80

Why does your night thief keep ambushing me,
Or lurking quietly in the long grass wait,
Sneak up on me to whisk away a friend?

Who says it's time for them to meet their end?
No rhyme or reason how you fix the date—
A random day or chosen by decree,

As one by one their number's up?
And why not me? Instead another one?
Please tell me this is not a mere caprice,

A cruel whim deciding who'll decease.
Declaring all the days of life now run,
You drain your psalmist's overflowing cup.

I ask and ask and yet you don't reply.
Why don't you answer now my plea,
As half in anger, half in broken prayer,

I'm crying out to you in my despair?
Why do you keep on doing this to me?
And still I'm yours in all my asking why.

81

Though I have to rise each time I fall
Learning every time I blip,
From each stumble, every slip,
Though I trust still in your longer haul,

Wasn't well enough best left alone—
Why then knock me off my stride?
I seemed so nearly home and dried,
Must I face afresh so much unknown?

How will I make my way in new terrain,
How anew to reach my pace?
Am I held in your embrace,
As I find my balance once again?

I, who was so steady on my feet,
Find my world turned on its head,
Sure of things but now instead
Powerless in my fall and my defeat.

Who'd decide to suffer, pay the price?
There's no choosing which growth pain;
Only in real loss is gain—
Loss by loss I gain your paradise.

82

Long before what's said and done,
You breathe in me and we conspire
So I return where I begin—
Your love both sends me out and draws
Me back, desires me to explore,
To find how to revert anew.

What you inspire I cannot shun,
No matter how with time I tire.
Is not to yearn the only sin?
You will forgive me all my flaws
And every failure you ignore
Once I remember my debut.

What was and what's to come are one,
Remembrance merging with desire
Still urges secretly within,
As your implanted promise gnaws;
Nostalgic now for all in store,
I'm homesick till I home in you.

83

So why postpone our heaven any more,
As though you sit determined to keep score

And all our joys to afterlife adjourn,
Accumulating points of bliss we earn?

Your glory's known in our own worldly things
As here on earth we fly with angels' wings.

The shame of losing you we also know—
We too have bitten dust and fallen low.

The kingdom here melds into kingdom come—
Your doom's day no payback by rules of thumb

Where good and bad we do are both rerun.
Both paradise and hell have long begun.

84

There was a time in youth to make our way,
To fight for space here underneath your sun
Where we can find ourselves and make our mark.

Our hurts and grudges nursed we now let go,
Old rivalries long wiped out by our years,
No longer worth the energy or fuss.

Outdated now our younger need to win.
No more it's one by one but side by side,
Our time too brief for rancour and mistrust.

What is the use to harbour dark within?
So many now have crossed the great divide—
Once bitter enmities have turned to dust.

Built-up resentments somehow fall away,
The tussles of our youth so long outrun,
In age we choose the light instead of dark.

Enlarged beyond a rigid long ago,
We're writing off all grievances' arrears.
Our God is rooming so much more in us.

85

All the skilled among you are to come
Making everything the Lord commands . . .
Decades we have spent on our career.

Service, yes, but do our egos lurk—
Driven discipline, ambition's thrust,
Merging with such skills we brought to bear?

Yet any pride we take you underwrite,
You insure our vain humanity,
Giving us our due once we serve you.

Taken with the task we had to do,
Focussed on our calling's need did we
Meanwhile miss so much of life's delight?

Let's so taste your pleasure's bill of fare
And to postponed excitements readjust—
Recreation's still creation's work.

May we a while enjoy just being here?
All undone we're leaving in your hands,
Learning now so sweetly to succumb.

86

Once we knew exactly who we were
When our own world was etched in black and white
And we were sure of what was right or wrong.

We knew who should and who should not belong—
The difference was as clear as day and night—
What reason could we have then to demur?

Always careful where to draw the line,
We knew how to avoid a step too far—
Was there really any cause to change

Still safe within our comfort zone and range
And certain all was either this or that,
An us and them was easy to define.

Was it a muddled need confused with doubt?
Still nervous we're betraying who we are,
Or that our thought and theirs must correspond,

We're drawn to understand your world beyond.
Expanding now our own thought's repertoire
We slowly have begun to open out.

But always the temptation to regress
Attempting somehow to reverse your plot,
And closing up our minds, no longer grow.

From noisy worlds that want to answer no,
Defining who we are by who we're not,
You lead us to the calmer time of yes.

87

You know how slowly we have earned success—
Don't knock us now because we're riding high;
Though in our triumph we are learning less,
Don't let your angels now come stealing by

To take what's more your gift than what we earned.
But burrowing through dark when we were tried
In all our trials one thing that we have learned
Is how we only ask and you decide

When we should lose so in our loss we gain,
And how through suffering's dark we best prevail.
But yet by choice we never seek out pain,
Although we know by times we need to fail.

Your light will dazzle in the tunnel's end;
Our brokenness is stronger in its mend.

88

Earthlings who have walked the moon we thought
Taming nature was our human role—
Surely it was ours to dominate.

Thinner now the ice on which we skate,
Nature keeps refusing our control;
Hubris could yet bring this world to nought.

Did we get above ourselves, believe
We deserve some privileged overview,
Stand outside so somehow we own all?

Now we're heading for a second fall,
Knowing no longer well as we once knew,
We depend on earth's own complex weave.

God, don't let all go so badly wrong!
We want to spend what we can never own—
If we change, is it too late at that?

Although our greed fouls up our habitat,
Teach us how we cannot thrive alone—
Earth we share is still where we belong.

89

Your wide world we so begrime,
Stumbling towards our own abyss.

Pardon how we plunder still
Driven by bored appetites;

Under burdens of rich greed
Out of kilter earth now groans.

Mother earth we know for sure
Can readjust to count us out,

Pummel us with floods or drought
Till our kind may not endure.

Now reclaiming too soft loans,
Pampered wishes more than need,

Earth no longer underwrites
Endless wants it can't fulfil.

God forgive our avarice,
Bring us down to earth in time.

90

The clicks of whales, the moaning cod,
The rabbit's thump, the squawking coot,
Each chortle, warble, cackle, growl,
All chirps and bleats, each purr and roar,
The shrieking owl and grunting boar,
Each coo and hum or whoop and howl,
The barks and bleats, each squeak and hoot,
Let everything that breathes praise God.

With every day begins anew
The secret murmurs of each soul,
The elephant who mourns a mate
Or lovers crying in their dreams,
Trees whispering where water streams
Conspiring soon to foliate
And ring a season in their bole
Are in their being praising you.

O teach us then to mend our ways!
How did we dare to think that we
Owned what breathes and blooms and so
Could reckon in our marketplace
The price of life on your earth's face?
Revering what exists we grow
And in relearned humility
Alongside all now feed you praise.

91

Our struggle to survive,
To tame, to learn, control
Enough so we'd endure

And find the drugs to cure
Disease, remake us whole,
Enough for us to thrive

And be your stewards here,
Still thankful and in awe
At how earth does your will,

All reconciled until
Accounts we overdraw
Begin to interfere.

An overreach for ease,
Control out of control,
Our skill without concern—

O help us to relearn
Our own attendant role,
Before the poles unfreeze,

Before a world unweaves.
But grown so ravenous
Can we somehow turn back

Before so out of whack
The earth will turn on us,
Your stewards turned now thieves?

Come tighten comfort's girth
Before it is too late,
Come free us from greed's grip

And teach us stewardship
Before our vandal fate
Lays waste to your sweet earth.

92

For all the mindless harm your humans do,
Your evolution's glory still is rife
With teeming, crawling, swimming life,
Whose busy dignity keeps praising you.

Though overmatched by all we need to mend
For every gift so grateful to the One,
While we yet breathe and soak your lavish sun,
Despair still is a self-besot dead-end.

One air, one water under your one sky—
No hiding now within our comfort zone,
All frontiers porous we are not alone,
As one together now we do or die.

For aftercomers, all we've yet to birth,
So help us God, we'll tend with love your earth.

93

You've seen extinctions come and go
Fin-backed reptiles, the dinosaur—
But didn't you at least intend

Us your humans to befriend
Earth that you'd let fail before?
Again this risked scenario

Here on our watch as some stand pat,
Head-in-sand and still deny
How ravenous we earthlings are.

Is this to take free will too far?
God, will you stand idly by
While we destroy our habitat?

Though through the eons long and slow
Arm's length is still your silent tact
That's racked by each mistake we make,

Desires we care for care's own sake,
Give us hands-on grace to act,
To save us from this touch and go.

94

How will it be when I start to decline?
Only you know what is in your design—
Yet so much more there is still to achieve.

Though I will take what extent you assign,
Please let me keep praising line after line,
Please let me love more before I must leave.

Sometimes, my God, look how I am afraid
Watching my friends older by a decade,
Growing so frail, shakier on their feet.

Now has begun beating such a retreat—
Long-reach recall day by day has outweighed
All that's close by, left all else in the shade.

If I need care, if I have to depend—
Please let old age then with wisdom combine
Making my praise an acceptance's sign.

Still to rejoice, never just to resign;
Grateful for what all this time has been mine,
Let me then go, giving thanks to the end.

95

Praise translucent leaves in early spring,
Laud just how the see-through water flows,
Bless the orange and yellow marigold,
All the bony trees that reach to hold
Darkly circling hooded homing crows.
Let us hallow you in everything—

Pounce-ready cats absorbing sun in bliss,
Whistling, clicking, pulsing humpbacked whales,
All that lopes and swings, that skips and leaps,

All that breathes and throbs and sweats and sleeps.
Every moment now our life inhales,
Thankful we share air with all of this.

96

But surely you're not cruel or unkind?
Why would this life which you both give and take
Be all? Why should you let us so evolve
That we cannot conceive oblivion,
Or how our being won't continue on?
We can't see how existence might dissolve,
Imagine sleep from which we wouldn't wake
Or conjure up an absence of our mind.

Although we know that clay returns to clay,
You knit our bones with carbon from the stars,
Their residue in us still heaven-high.
Why fill us with your sweet eternal dream
If everything you knit you soon unseam?
If there is nothing more beyond so why
This hope and this belief that you've made ours?
All these desires could you then just betray

And leave us in oblivion's no-man's-land?
Our doubts attack what we can't apprehend,
As dust, as grass, as flowers in the field
The wind blows over us and we are gone.
Yet carbon dust in stars that once had shone
Will yearn for what you've promised, not revealed.
For all complaining doubt still in the end,
You know we trust though we can't understand.

97

Yes sometimes I wondered as I grew
If you had to smile at needs to achieve,
To climb, to surpass, to win, to score,

Our need to access and measure how far
We'd come, to be first, the alpha plus.
But why are there still awards not won?

Success is a star-high greasy pole,
There always beyond some prize to gain;
Again to succeed the reason why

One victory more will satisfy
Excitement still in life's fastest lane,
But why is all stardom this black hole?

We slowly learn all said and done,
It's who we have loved and who loved us
Allows us a glimpse of the God you are

And know in the end how there's nothing more—
All totted and balanced before we leave,
The sum of our success is loving you.

98

So miniscule the moment we abide,
A nothing in five billion years of days.
A hundred thousand million stars above—
But in their eons do we leave a trace
In passing on a rumour from afar?

Down age to age our history's thin thread
In all who plough, who till, who sow, who reap,
In those who stumble, struggle to endure,
Who grind, who sweat, who toil and drudge to live,
Who sing and dance and love, who laugh and cheer

While slowly day-by-day becomes each year,
Extends its long genetic narrative
As cradle-rockers night-feed to ensure
New generations will too laugh and weep
And carry on desires of all the dead.

Across millennia of laps we are
Your baton-passers in this human race
As we relay our rumour of your love.
Infinitesimal, our lives still praise;
In magnifying you we're magnified.

99

Do we abandon you so we can learn
That though we feed on Eden's contraband
And think we're masters of the universe
Who'll find the perfect way to conquer all,
A thousand years for you is just a day
Awaiting prodigals who choose to home?

How thinking somehow we'd outgrown you,
We're in our inwardness so self-obsessed
We oust you from our world and then instead
Revere meandering mazes of the mind;
Or sure we have the perfect plan, dictate,
Expending lives on dogma's altar stone.

Although we'd thought that everything was known,
We can't tie down the dance your quarks create.
Watch over us your boastful humankind
Who in our pride had once declared you dead
And out of greed have fouled our finespun nest
And done so much we cannot now undo.

You don't extract a price because we roam,
No borrowed pride we must in turn repay—
Instead you still forgive our every fall
And your forbearance eases Eden's curse,
Allows us all our time to understand
We leave to love you more on our return.

100

Hand down the theme
But make it seem
It's ours to make our own,
Our leitmotif to intercede,

Take up the tune
As we commune,
A follower or lead,
On beat and in the zone.

But passed a phrase
We'll each amaze
With what's unplanned yet sure—
A solo line can't show a doubt.

In wordless prayer
Of jazz we dare
Like children to cry out
So what's within emerges pure.

No chance to sham—
Our time to jam
And give your theme full range.
Let each of us in turn obsess

Enough to soar
Beyond before
And show in playfulness
Your endless appetite for change.

No note foretold,
Let riffs unfold
And in the groove allow
The unpredicted to astound.

Under your eyes
We improvise
Democracies of sound
To praise you in the jazz of now.

101

O you who once took love away
Yet gave me still the strength to bear
The pain of what was not to be,
I heard you hearing every prayer
As listening to my broken plea,
You held my hopelessness at bay
When you assuaged my loneliness
And matched my grief with your caress.

Always I give you thanks and pray.
But though I know that you were there
To hold me in love's filigree;
And though again I walk on air,
For all my talk and buoyancy,
O yes, my feet are made of clay
And I rely on your largesse—
Please still keep watch when I regress.

So though this morning's world turns grey
And leaden mists exude despair;
As gloom comes sneaking up on me
To catch my psyche unaware
And trap me in its ennui,
Don't let a soul you buoyed fall prey
To dust and temptress nothingness.
This is a morning you must bless.

102

Your glow will never cease from breaking through,
It's shaping all we'll bring you since our birth;
Your many-mansion house we now preview.
For as it is in heaven, so on earth.

Does all existence revel in our growth?
A world below, a world beyond you splice
So glories of your realm can sweep up both—
Your earth and heaven bask in paradise.

You burnish us with pain for brighter joy,
A radiance we'll bring with us above;
All gifts enhanced, all talents we deploy
Prepare us to enrich your heaven's love.

So as it is on earth in heaven too.
You shine in us as we will shine in you.

103

Why does such self-reproach still gnaw inside?
Although we glory in how things evolved,
Old ghosts come back to haunt a house rebuilt;
Emerging in small hours to disconcert,
Regrets will come to blame us face to face.

Transgressions that can never be reversed
Return to spook our fragile self-regard;
Our image of ourselves forever marred
At best by grief, by deep remorse at worst.

As lovers in each other's arms embrace
Both pasts and slowly heal what's bruised or hurt,
Enfold us, wipe away our nagging guilt;
For though we trust misdeeds are long absolved,
God, help us to forgive our wounded pride.

104

There were times I thought my words were mine
Believed I spoke instead of you in me;
But fleeing you I heard pride's Doppler shift,
My change of pitch rang false in both our ears.

Was it prophetic haste, ambition's itch,
That let us so forget humility,
A terror we might join the losing class?

Yet things we dream that never come to pass,
The milk and honey lands not meant to be
Command our ears to hear your perfect pitch.

All nagging fears of failure die with years.
Your mouth in mine, I'm steward of your gift;
All promised lands I know I'll never see
Remind me how I owe you every line.

105

You, God, are one– no counterpart,
And doublemindedness won't do.

When here before the First and Last,
In front of the Unique, the One,

Distractions melt. We do not dare
What's frivolous but speak instead

Our deepest needs, the needs of all
We hope your love might underwrite.

Once single-minded in your sight
Our pretensions seem so small.

All daily ostentation shed
Then in your presence we prepare

A final letting-go when done
With all fame gathered, things amassed,

Our whole life's gift returns to you,
Your oneness lived with all our heart.

106

Should we who can keep working to the end?
And will there always be so much to do—
Some other way discovered to extend
Ourselves, new barriers worth breaking through?

We strive through life to serve a greater good;
As labour is our joy, we do not shirk
But give our all in doing all we should—
Surely God by now accepts our work?

Though in our calling, yes, of course we praise
And rightly we rejoice in each success;
Yet in the end it's how we love that weighs,
All those by whom we're blessed and those we bless.

We eat our bread and in life's wine delight
To bask in love's sweet warmth by day and night.

107

How should I pray to you,
Entreat you to fill
My being with your harmony?
Will you not teach
How to beseech
You, God, implore you to instil
Serenity in me?

No need to act or do.
Please make a monk of me
Who in his quietude delights.
Alone I'll muse,
A silent schmooze
With you in that tranquility
Allowed to anchorites.

Such peace is overdue.
But though such silence calms,
I must blurt out my thanks anew—
The only way
I know to pray
Turns all stillness into psalms
To praise and hallow you.

108

All hail our loving impresario!
You cast and trust how in the longer haul
We play the roles we're given in the show,
Yet prompt us for the final curtain fall.

In age our long-term memory prevails,
Consigns our recent life to second place,
Allows the past to tip our recall's scales,
Unbalance us and catch our minds off base.

So vivid on our recollection's screen,
Those images we caught with childhood's eye
Seem more intense than they had ever been
As though outdoing years that they belie.

Is this perspective shift within the brain
Our soul-deep need to summon up once friends
Who drifted where we never meet again?
Is this a kind of tying up of ends?

But seeing, knowing, understanding all,
Have you our human hard wire so designed,
That you rehearse for us our curtain call,
Ensure we bring the whole cast back to mind?

You concentrate our memory's liquid screen
So making sure we actors now prepare
To recognise all from our childhood scenes
In heaven's grand revival's première.

109

Tent-dweller, nomad in no-man's-land,
For all the bricks and spires
Of our desires,
You still withstand
All housing that will wall you in.

Why, why do we so want then to pin
You down? We can't contain
Or ever rein
Your being in
That's nowhere and still everywhere.

Charged spirit energy can just flare—
A high-voltage flash
Of love's panache
Attending prayer.
You are, God extraordinaire,

All present. So no need now to care.
We, letting go
With your flow,
Can everywhere
Deep in your nowhere rest in you.

110

You're here when we toast
Foretaste hereafter,

Here where friends meet,
Here when we laugh.

Your glance in each face
At our table's feast

Glimmering and yet so clear,
A glimpse in those who've been

Listening as we grew,
All those who wisely heard,

Blessed dreams in embryo,
See how we still can grow.

So taken at our word,
Somehow in trusting you

We trust how we are seen.
Gone inhibition and fear.

Each for the other priest
As here we now embrace.

Here as we quaff,
Here as we eat,

You're topping up laughter,
Invisible host.

111

Love leaves love behind,
One bereft of love,
Bitten but not shy.

Fearsome bush now burn,
Whirlwind speak out loud,
We must question you,

We must have our say!
Why afflict us so,
Salt old lonely sores?

Who laid out the skies?
All that's wild may stun,
Trust me thick and thin.

Who willed the world to spin?
Who stoked up the sun?
Trust how I surprise!

Love's a grace that pours
Manna's honeyed snow,
Wilderness sorbet,

Out of God's own blue—
Glorious ninth cloud,
Joy we can't adjourn.

There's no asking why
Push returns to shove.
Love is wild and blind.

112

Relying so on you and yet to scare,
Allow both fret and fray to domineer;
A lover in a dangerous affair,
Belief so veers between both trust and fear.

This life so beautiful, this life so wild
Unfolds its risks in every lovely breath;
A trust and mistrust never reconciled
That's both unravelled and fulfilled in death.

Yet no controlling when or where or why.
What is it worth then to obsess or fuss?
Worst case scenario is not to die,
Far worse that you should turn your face from us.

Beyond all else to need your love to live,
We're craving for what's only yours to give.

113

I bless you God although I don't know how
To thank enough for air, for light, for food.
I do not take for granted—I receive.

Some evenings on the streets I walk on air
And so light-heartedly, so full of hope
I feed you praise, shout out my thanks to you

Who knows the inner light and shade in me,
The chiaroscuro where trust turns to fear,
Afraid of age and loss, afraid to die.

O answer me and listen to my cry,
Just reassure me, tell me that you hear!
I yearn for you for all eternity.

In griefs you gave I deepened and came through.
Then come the time, then come the grace to cope,
Let trust in you refuse all blind despair

And heaven start on earth where by your leave,
Here in between my hope and gratitude,
I bless you God in your eternal now.

114

How much can younger years of ours foresee?
And even what they see they cannot heed—
Impatience always doubts your best intent.

So many times I thought you thwarted me
When dreams so near seemed only to recede.
So easy to grow bitter and resent

How you forbid the fruit of Eden's tree,
Withholding triumphs that seem guaranteed—
Yet blessings you disguise are heaven sent.

So much we hadn't wished was meant to be—
Though sure we failed when hoping to succeed,
We find we're glad all went just as it went.

Absolved, fulfilled, amazed we are now free.
What could we lack? You've given all we need
To praise, to thank, to bless and be content.

115

How could you not deplore our foolish wrongs
When we have missed the mark or we misaim
The love we know is ours to aim for you.

And yet you, God, who never cast a stone,
Refusing blank to harbour any grudge,
Don't file our sins in heavenly archives.

You are the nurturer who sees mistakes
But separating doer from the deed
Can love what's good and so dismiss the breach

As insecurities and overreach;
And still our parent watching for our need
You see our weakness, suffer for our sakes.

However wrongs may dog us in our lives,
Uninterested in sin, no blackcap judge,
To love you well again is to atone.

We each begin and rebegin anew,
By nature not defined by guilt or shame,
For all misdeeds, a child who still belongs.

116

God, you are my love and I say yes,
I am yours for better or for worse.

Though you know I praise when all is well,
Yet even in my anguish I extol,

Glorify the one I have and hold.
Try as you will, I'll love you more.

Not just things I think that I require—
Happiness now larger than I know;

Dreams I dreamed already I outgrow,
We are yours, whatever you desire.

Free from whims and fears I can adore,
Trust that you who all my love enfold,

Though desiring every living soul,
Doom cold evildoers to their hell.

To the end this vow we will rehearse—
God, you are my love and I say yes.

117

Half-understanding we know how
To tinker with, to thimblerig
Your world and half-aware infringe
On nature, turning wealth to dearth.

Too clever now by half we may
Be wiped from mother earth's sweet face—
A button pressed, atomic leaks;
We know so much yet are not wise.

We know each figure and each fact,
Our skills, high-tech all holding sway—
Where is a wisdom of the heart
To question what we are about?

We cannot piously opt out,
On earth's stage still our earthling's part—
Let's act as if we cannot pray
And pray as if we cannot act.

Though knowing who laid out the skies,
Excited by all new techniques,
Without reflection we keep pace
With recklessness we still obey.

But show us again this planet earth
You hung on understanding's hinge;
Though for our boots we grow too big,
From unwise knowing save us now.

118

Part of human fate
Half-aware chagrin,
Cravings deep within

Somehow to make sense,
Find whatever might
Sate an appetite,

Gnawing that's innate,
Hunger for an aim,
Purposes to frame

Our sojourn on earth,
Which both fame and wealth
Bid to give by stealth.

Market blandishments
Seek still to inspire
All we must acquire,

Fill our dreams with greed,
Dreaming to have more.
Empty as before,

Teach us our own worth—
Only love assures
How we still are yours.

You are our one need,
All that we require.
You are our desire.

119

What drives our tiny lives to climb above?
In our need
To succeed,
To get on top, to dominate, to win
We compete, we contend,
At any cost we shin the greasy pole.
Does winner take all?

Still everywhere outsiders' cries
From below,
From skid row,
To ask why we must further dispossess
Down or out, weak and frail,
All left behind.

Less deaf than blind
Teach again compassion's braille
So growing in an open brokenness
We in turn
Also learn
How earthed in what rich despise

We never fall.
Confessing our own weakness we are whole
So we know in the end
How only such assuredness within
Can ensure
Can secure
All futures in your reckless love.

120

You stole a lifelong love of mine,
Uprooted half my history—
I know the winter of your ways.

But how could I have known,
That what was deep could deepen more,
Re-rooting in re-harrowed ground?

You understood the longer haul,
Foreseeing all I couldn't see,
Hollowed out by loss and grief,

I'd sow in tears, then bear the sheaf
Of your unending mystery,
A signal and a hope for all.

The joy of what was lost re-found.
As fruits that ripen to their core
Two hearts that wintered once alone

Now tend impassioned summer days.
Let such late seasoned love then be
In this our broken world your sign.

121

No in between, your choice is stark,
You show us both the dark and light
And though in dawn and dusk they blend,
Just one will gain the upper hand,
Invade the other till it cedes.

Yet you allow the dark success,
Let wrongers thrive and have their day
And in greed's hugger-mugger room
Intrigue and scheme how to supplant
Whoever dares to thwart their will.

Are we who love you too blue-eyed,
Too innocent to comprehend
How others do not want your light,
Imagine demons that can drive
Such lust for wealth and power and fame?

We cannot beat them at their game—
Although we guess how they connive,
We still can lack the will to fight
Malevolence that they intend
Our need to love you half-denied.

And yes, we bank on you yet still
You are no short-term God. We can't
Forget when hidden by the gloom
What's wicked too has power and sway
As seeded in their hopelessness

Their hotbed of despair still breeds
An evil we can't understand.
Determined to the bitter end
We trust through all the pitch of night,
Your dazzling still will banish dark.

122

In your world how much we could lament,
All loss, all pain, all angst we could bewail,

Complain how you allow creation crush
Already brief and fragile lives you gave,

Bemoan a storm, a flood, a drought, a quake.
How seeing all of this must we sit tight,

Not even ask you to at least explain,
Wait out in trust millennia of years?

But you respond in hints and signs and clues,
In courting lovers walking hand in hand,

Who dream new life that nature will demand,
Whose whispers let the leap of spring suffuse

Birches' buds that break in mouses' ears
And grow to see-through leaves in sunlit rain.

In love again with life we in delight
Re-cry the tears we cried in our heartache.

For all the grief and loss from crib to grave,
Your world so sweet, so full, so rich, so lush

That trembling on joy's soaring Richter scale
We rebegin our paradise ascent.

123

Free us from a guilt that gnaws,
A spy so treasonous,
An enemy within,
Recalling all our flaws,
Recounting each and every sin
And raking from our past
Transgressions that still cast
First stones at us.

Free us from our shadow fear
That tracks our every thought
While stalking all our hours
To sleuth and domineer,
A private eye who disempowers
With angst and dread,
Awake or in our bed
All life is fraught.

Free us from that nag self-doubt—
That inner advocate
Examines us to try
To find us out,
A self-accusing inward eye
That countermines self-trust
Until we think we must
Now fail or quit.

Free us from what hems us in,
From all that can debar
Us from life's sheer delight.
Let heaven now begin
As eternity takes flight
More daring and secure
On wings that know for sure
How loved we are.

124

By times I speak as 'I', by times as 'we'—
But you, my God, will know exactly why,
Know how I know I entered with a cry
And will as likely end as I began.

But in between we are dependent too,
We're living in each other's light and shade
And so I have become myself amidst
All friends and loves allowing me be me.

Yet I've no use for false humility—
I know my gift but am no egoist;
In every word I've spoken I have prayed,
I am in others' service here for you.

One tiny life, yet in your love I span
All in your world now sighing in my sigh,
Humanity cries out though I say 'I',
I cry for us in my intensity.

125

An infant cry in us in full defence
Of buried fears and deepest wounds within
Demands success of us to recompense
Some memory of loss that craves to win.

How is it the oppressed, the poor, the maimed,
The broken with so little left to lose,
Allow us name a weakness never named
And let us show each inner wound and bruise?

For each of us is hiding deep inside
A loneliness that only you appease;
Though often we dissemble out of pride,
Our owning our fragility brings ease.

A peace rewrites our wounded life's memoir,
Your endless love fulfilling who we are.

126

I will thank you for the choice
To come or go at will;
You never could instil
In us devotion as you're the God who gave
Us freedom of desire—
I am the faithful lover you invite.

No, of course, you do not want
Affection by demand
Or love that you'd command
And so prefer to risk that we'd say no.
But offering all I crave
I've fallen for the One who needs to dare.

Head over heels sweet nothings now my prayer,
I share with you my heart's enclave,
All secret fears of age and letting go,
Despite your promised land.
But do you understand
God, my friend, my confidant?

My soul has percolated your delight—
Don't test me now with fire
You know how I'm afraid I won't be brave
If put through suffering's mill.
I dread all pain yet still
In my fear I will rejoice.

127

Good morning, God! A lavish sun ablaze
Caresses us and warms our marrow bones.

So much to do, so many things to tend
That stake in turn their claim and counterclaim

On all these sweetest hours that stretch ahead,
On precious minutes shading off our time.

Now in the silence of what's left undone
Here in the sabbath of a sun-drenched space,

Content to bask in your unseen embrace
Where surely good and happiness are one,

We sense how indolently sound can climb
To unheard heights. All inhibition shed,

With our imperfect pitch we hum your name
And partials rise, harmonics that ascend

Where joy sends up to you its overtones.
Delight has set this day aside for praise.

128

At last we're certain we've arrived.
Though we've always strived
To intervene
Where unbeknownst we've always been
Since birth
Both in heaven and on earth.

Your kingdom has already come
Where we can succumb,
And know that each
Of us while here below can reach
Above.
Our reality your love

Above as below, where now
When we still allow
Your will be done
Eternity and now are one
And we
Had never plucked your Eden's tree.

My years begin to mount and I
Now no longer try
To counter you.
Let things just happen as I do
Your will.
Perhaps some dreams I won't fulfil,

Ambitions I may not achieve,
Work that I will leave
Undone. All time
Is yours and in your kingdom I'm
At ease
With whatsoever may still please.

I'm freer than I've ever been,
Wild and yet serene;
Come day, go day,
See how I dare in work or play
Let go.
I'm trusting you who are the flow.

129

You are the playwright still whose stage we hold
And improvise our lines to fit your plot,
Where you who know the craft will only show
By hints and cues or letting us explore
The overall magnificence in you.

The sun was once a spotlight touring us
Before we learned our earth's much humbler role
And telescopes revealed your galaxies
Where heavens stretch imagination's scale
Beyond what is beyond our mind's eye's range.

The flies above, the trap room down below
Where atoms were the currency of things,
A swirl of quarks excites our prying mind
And mysteries of smallness stay in play
To match the whirl of galaxies on high.

And in between on stage we wonder why
So silently you gave us humans sway
Whom you still covenant yet never bind,
But in your goodness prompt us from the wings.
How big our parts, how little all we know.

No neat dénouement you prearrange
Yet present in your absence you unveil
A grandeur you keep showing by degrees;
From space-time foam to each black hole,
Creation's scope so rich and copious.

All we discover leads us cue by cue,
No scene can leave things as they were before
And each act is the next in embryo;
But still the drama of not knowing what
In theatres of your glory we unfold.

130

Don't try us out the way you once tried Job—
A better man and made of sterner stuff—

The more you delve the deeper you now probe,
The more we hope that we'll have grit enough

To trust in you, our God, no matter what,
To have the fortitude if things get rough,

When you will know if we are yours or not
Or if our trust was nothing but our bluff.

Yet strange how suffering never undermines
A lifelong trust's inherent come-what-may;

The more we trust the more your glory shines,
Your splendour growing in such interplay;

The more you dig the deeper love becomes
As if all suffering makes the depths it plumbs.

131

Though you do anything you want
Still you would not force your love,
But I am chosen to believe.

You wooed me with life's opulence,
Courted me out of your need,
Pursued me so relentlessly.

Though your desire can come on strong,
A while I played hard to get
And so gave you the run around

Before I dared to open up,
Before I told you I was yours
And blurted out my faith in you.

All faith is surely also love,
Delight feeding on delight
That won't explain its when or why

Or how it grows in dailiness,
Thriving on attentiveness,
A passionate yet steady flame.

You're changing and extending me
In ways I had not foreseen
Beckoning me beyond myself

Into those depths of who you are
I'm not made to understand;
And yet you keep inviting me,

Drawing me into mysteries
Which although in love I name,
Still with wonder my voice so soft.

132

On the move we never gather moss—
Each biography a rolling stone.

Facing all that's strange we say good-bye,
Take our leave of all when certain how

Things should be to hold our world in place.
Can we tell you, God, what you should do?

Something deep in us resents all change,
Yet we know we must begin our slow

Re-adaption and our letting-go.
Lives we learn in loss to rearrange

Mourn the brokenness that births what's new.
Every unknown is a chance embrace,

Every change a death that may allow
Cries in us to hear another's cry

Asking us to make all grief our own.
Show us, God, abundance in our loss.

133

In watches of the night dread grips the soul
When hampered by our fear we do not dare

Envision what's beyond our own control
Or trust in our God's own panache and flair.

So hemmed in, our hearts in disarray,
That overcome we barely still can care;

In dim-lit anguish we might seize the day
Or fall into a black hole of despair.

Instead a star that dark may not destroy
Or force at whim to flicker half and half,

A world in us that feared bursts out in joy
Where in distress we're licensed still to laugh—

The grace of hope is each decision made
To love the light where we are not afraid.

134

Some love you from childhood on,
Cherish you through all their youth

And year by faithful year still yours
Through lifetimes you are their all,

Others here and now crave power,
Fame and wealth at any cost;

If turning to you they repent,
You atone for all they rue.

Still most of us are in between—
Not evildoer, not saint—

Who in our youth left you behind,
In our bloom had veered from you;

But steered to you returned again,
Approaching you in hope anew,

Nurturing trust we'd broken once
Mending bonds we'd breached in haste.

You love creation come what may,
No matter what we are your own,

Who is there you cannot forgive?
You may pardon all you will.

Your mercy stretches to our end
Even to a death-bed change.

We're each of us your protégé—
Love us all your venial brood.

135

Maybe at first a kind of bet,
Gambling on a God that is

A God whose only proof is time,
Belief that's lived in day by day

As every mood and tone is shared,
Humour's every whim revealed,

All joys, all pain, all shame, all love,
Our praise, anger, griefs and hopes,

Until our history takes root.
A present that still owns a past,

Emits its rays of surety,
Underpinning confidence

That you record our every day.
You remember all our lives,

Attentive suitor that you are,
A lover constantly aware

Until what seemed a wager laid,
A guess made, a chance we took

Embeds a faith in who you are,
And shares a trust of layered years.

136

But why do you still let us suffer so,
Watch over our affliction from afar

And force us to cry out in our despair
To you who in your silence won't respond,

Though desperation knocks on heaven's gate?
Do you not know that we belong to you

Or how we glorify you all our days,
Assured that in your sight our lives are blest

Until you strike when we are happiest,
Afflicting us who always chose to praise?

How can we sing that every morning's new?
How can we say your faithfulness is great,

Believe beyond where there seems no beyond,
Or even hope that you in heaven care?

And still I trust the mystery you are.
Surprise me, God, with what I can't yet know.

137

Should I be your Jeremiah,
Voice and prophet of a doom?

The ice now thaws, our earth will burn,
Your creation all askew.

Should I warn of our false gods?
Should I name our golden calves,

Tell how we are so sick at heart
Who still gratify desire,

Indulge ourselves no matter what?
Tomorrow's grief that day's care,

Our graven image here and now,
Our idol such a god of greed.

Can we learn to do with less,
Sacrifice a need for ease,

Renew with you our covenant?
Inscribe in us your love's own pact.

In you let all that is be one.
Turn rapacious hearts to you.

138

Each day do you create the world anew?
You do not want a once-off paradigm—
So urged by you to face both joy and pain,
We stumble on still learning to relearn
How from each fall a child in us can rise.

We fall and yet your Eden's never far,
For even if with guile we second guess
Or doubt when tried how we can still revert
To taste a fruit the sweeter for our loss,
Surprised we find we rise again to soar

Before you choose to test our love once more.
Although our purposes may seem to cross,
You still intend to mend us with each hurt,
For somehow in our broken openness,
The nearer you, the more childlike we are.

As though our lives advance contrariwise
We see each ordeal through and then return
And yet we don't regress but rather gain
An innocence more glorious each time;
Each day a process journeys towards you.

139

From Adam onwards we have known
Human days are like the grass,

We flourish as a field of flowers
And wither like the green herb.

Remember man that thou art dust
And to dust thou wilt return.

We have a million million nerves
Abuzz with crisscross messaging

To grow and flourish and mature,
Then fade and die and feel no more.

Belief in you is in your gift,
A trust above and beyond,

In face of what our reason says.
For all seeming nothingness,

A love hid in the word belief
Shapes a sweet eternity

That shines in faces of close friends,
As daring laughter's giddy time

We learn to hear you sight unseen,
Your hushaby begetter's voice

Assuring us that all is well.
Surely, God, you would not lie?

140

Your world is surely heaven's overflow,
Abundance of delight decanting love,
Excess of being, spillage from above
Desiring others' joy from your word go.

Why such angst among those spoilt for choice,
Disquietude that haunts a rootless mind?
And in stale knowingness now flying blind
Will no one any longer dare rejoice?

Our happiness the daily now and here,
A greeting kiss, an evening meal prepared,
The humdrum bliss of news and memories shared
When with and for each other we cohere.

Your joy hides in this worldly every day,
The sweet mundane where heaven still holds sway.

141

You are our great risk-taking God
Who gambles on being loved.

You knew how fickle we could be,
How unfaithful lovers stray—

But yours is sheer daredevilry,
Flouting all the odds we'd cheat.

O wanting God, for all your power,
You lay your love still on the line,

For who'd command a faithful heart,
Who'd enjoy devotion forced?

You let desire beget delight
Which in turn gives more desire

As all the while you will forgive
Stumbling processes of love.

Although you are betrayed or spurned,
Still our God who seeks and yearns.

142

Forgive my brief communiqués,
Pardon me your absentee,

So absorbed by incarnate love,
Wrapped up in life's overflow.

My prayers are interjected thanks,
Lauding how things are and were

Or my attempts to intercede,
Ombudsman for all who lack.

Sometimes I dare to supplicate,
Asking more than you've designed,

But time and time again I find
My desires all out of date,

What seemed my way a cul-de-sac.
You know better what I need—

To what you will I will defer,
My desires your love outflanks.

What you want for me I know
My plans can fall so short of.

I pray for all you will for me,
Then return to thanks and praise.

143

Who is this one that we keep talking to,
The one who's everywhere and yet afar,
The loved unseen whose energies imbue
A swirling universe from quark to star?

Who is this suitor we kneel down to praise,
Whose face we living never can behold?
Who is this lover who can so amaze,
We mystery by mystery unfold?

Is all creation one love-letter sent
To hold us in our wonder's lovesick thrall—
The atom's whirl, the blackholed firmament
As aeons flirt across time's cosmic hall?

In quarks below, in galaxies above,
You write the mathematics of your love.

144

How can we think of such infinity,
A world without beginning or an end,
Our yearning's lifelong sought magnetic pole,
A God whose love is every day's fresh start?

How can we see what slips beyond our speech?
What's infinite eludes our finite sound;
Each psalm a symbol's half, a broken sign,
Where words allude to what the heart has seen.

Though metaphors fall short of our desire,
There's still some burning need in us to tread
Where even angels fear to offer signs.
Our symbols by their nature will conceal

What at once they're trying to reveal
By letting silence point behind the lines
To where the heart may see what can't be said,
A glory glanced to which our hearts aspire.

Imagination hovers in-between
If sight and sound can somehow realign
And two halves come together in the round,
Two matching parts that mend a symbol's breach.

Once we glimpse a token's counterpart
And eye the two part symbol as a whole,
Such seeing is believing's dividend,
Our fragile lives transformed by all we see.

145

Our happiness a choice
To still rejoice,
No matter what or where

To face with valiance
How years advance—
So here's my daily prayer

That somehow I'll be wise
And hear all cries
Then serve with tenderness;

That I with joy can share
What's yours, aware
How better more than less.

Show me the golden mean
The yes between
Sore lack and sour excess.

Let love's dynamo
Drive all. Although
Time's ashen hand ungloved

Now thumbs its dust to dust,
You know I trust
I love and still am loved.

146

Today your Adam lives anew,
Knows this world is here for him—

The high and azure sky above,
Sunlight in the river flows,

Oak trees fluttering summer leaves,
A terrace of marigolds,

Berries stacked on a street fruit stall
Plump black, red and blue display.

Who'd be a puritan today?
Who'd not want to savour all?

This is Eden. A world unfolds
Gardens where no fruit deceives,

Where in your light creation glows.
Here's my life and I'm in love!

Your glory overflows its brim.
All that is calls us to you.

147

O God, what fools we are
Who scar
Your earth and wound a planet's bone and flesh,
Unravelling rashly mesh by mesh
A habitat's intricateness,
Creation's own complex finesse.

As bodies compensate,
Create
A slouch to match a limp's lopsidedness,
So too your planet will redress
As best it can what's out of whack
But negative loops keep feeding back.

Will ice-melts flood the earth?
A dearth
Of shining surface mirroring the sun
Ensures your earth has now begun
To soak up sun and in turn cause
A grander scale of Arctic thaws

And gases icecaps stow
Below
Escape to hang a sky-high canopy
Which radiation cannot flee,
So vicious circles self-fulfil—
What had warmed is warmer still.

But why will no one see
How we
And your enfolded biosphere are one
Here under your dwarf yellow sun?
Our planet craves your slow caress.
Restore us to inwovenness.

148

Which of us when young did not believe
Our sap and juices always would prevail?
In spring's lush green how could we ever fail?
Is there a dream that youth cannot achieve?

To be in health and strength is not to think,
To take it all as given as the air;
Just as we breathe entirely unaware,
Why should unconscious vigour ever sink?

How brief our body's innocent leasehold
Before the psalmist now returns on cue
To whisper in our ear a plea to you:
Do not cast me away when I am old.

Whatever time you in your wisdom give,
I wake, I choose, I taste, I love, I live.

149

But why conceal a talent's light
Or hide it in a bushel's dark?

Why should we be such broken reeds,
Our head hung low, our doubting will

Afraid if we should make our mark
That you might see us as too proud?

You want no fake humility
That falsely leaves a gift unused,

For surely you, our God, will bless
A level-headed giddiness.

As modesty and pride confused
Denies our lives their apogee.

Please let me talk to you out loud—
I crave the thrill, your sacred spark,

Embrace my gift's unhurried skill,
Sweet patience of perfection's needs.

As brother's keeper, as your clerk,
I praise and hold your world in flight.

150

From life's start we endure
By fight or flight where fit survive
For more than some four billion years.

Are our hearts in arrears?
How can humankind now thrive
Unless evolving we mature.

Greed commands, lust for power
Discounts creation's weak or frail—
Those who have still want it all.

One we stand, split we fall;
We cannot be allowed to fail—
We've reached our own eleventh hour.

Ice still thaws. Oceans rise
What rainforests have we felled?
There's plastic in the snows that fall,

Noah's floods over all
And summer heat unparalleled.
Show us how yet we might be wise!

Ravens no! Send a dove!
Bring us back a flood-high twig,
And shun warmongers' stoked up fears.

From our mouth to God's ears!
Teach us with the olive sprig
To cherish faults in all we love.

Name it then God's success
How we evolve to understand
The freedom of unselfish care.

Grant us now grace to dare
Your evolution's fresh demand;
To love the weak your love's finesse.

GOSPEL

ZECHARIAH

Red-letter day, once only in his life,
As righteous Zechariah the priest is let
Offer incense, his whole world's upset
When told how Elizabeth his barren wife

Will bear a son and they must name him John.
Filled with the spirit, never drinking wine,
He will be great before our God, a sign
Bringing joy and gladness from now on,

And in Elijah's power and spirit go
Before the Lord. He doubts the things he hears.
An old man, my wife well on in years,
How can I know, he asks, that this is so?

With doubts and fears this priest is overcome—
Could all this happen to a son of his?
In disbelief now Zechariah is
Until the day these things occur struck dumb.

In time a son is born and mercy shown
As God has heard Elizabeth's aged plea,
And Zechariah has his eyes to see
What if he had not doubted he'd have known.

Elizabeth will name him John but none
Before was John—this flouts their naming rite;
But still dumbfounded let the father write
Whatever name he wants now for his son.

Before the angel he had been nonplussed—
Was pregnant silence Zechariah's pace?
His name is John. The Lord has shown a grace
And letters dare what words had feared to trust.

Luke's gospel tells how this would so amaze
All there as God unfolds what he'd decreed.
A mouth is opened and a tongue is freed;
Undammed a muteness overflows in praise.

ANNUNCIATION

The day the angel Gabriel was sent,
Although he must have known she would consent,

He was aware he came out of the blue.
'Rejoice you gracious one, the Lord's with you!'

Yes, Mary was confused and wondered why
This greeting, pondered what it must imply

That he had given her this accolade.
The angel said to her, 'Be not afraid

'For Mary, you are God's own favoured one
And now you will conceive and bear a son

'Who will be Jesus, Son of the Most High
Whose kingdom has no end'. She asks, 'Since I

'Am still a virgin, how then can this be?
How could this ever come about for me?'

He tells her what the One on High will do—
'The spirit's power will overshadow you'.

'Here I am the servant of the Lord;
Be it with me according to your word'.

NATHANAEL

First Jesus ran
Into Philip—as told by John—
The day he chose to go to Galilee,
Where those he'd called already came from too.

Here Jesus said to Philip, 'Follow me'.
Now Philip found Nathanael who was
Then told how Jesus was the one
The prophets and Mosaic law foretold.

'From out of Nazareth can any good
Now come? From Jesus who is Joseph's son?'
Nathanael will ask. 'O surely none!'
But Philip answered him, 'If you just would

'Come meet him for yourself. So come and see!'
'There comes a guileless man', now Jesus said.
'How could you know me yet?' he asks. 'Ahead
Of Philip's call, I saw you there beneath a tree'.

In shocked belief here Philip's names are bold:
'You're Israel's king and God's own son'.
But Jesus asks, 'Do you believe because
I said I saw you under your fig tree?

'For greater things you'll see I tell all you—
The heavens opened, God's angels you will see
Ascending and descending on
The Son of Man'.

TWELVE

He called the twelve and sent them two by two—
Now heaven's kingdom near, proclaim all new!

Plainspoken men with ordinary names,
A Simon, Thomas, Philip, John or James

Just told what they got free they'll give away.
Whatever house they enter there they'll stay;

No journey bag, a worker earns his food—
But if unwelcome or in his name pursued,

Their peace returned to them, they should retreat
And shake that town's dust off their sandalled feet.

Cure sick, raise dead, cast evil spirits out.
But were they sure or did they know self-doubt?

A taxman, zealot, thief and fishermen
In this new world so far beyond their ken

Must be afraid if beaten they'll give way.
If brought before the courts what would they say

Or dragged before the governors and kings
Would they embrace Christ's promised sufferings,

Instead of eye for eye turn trusting cheeks,
Believe through them a father's spirit speaks?

HOMETOWN

O yes throughout Galilee but if
A prophet comes uninvited now,
Returns to his hometown Nazareth
And chooses to read Isaiah's scroll—
The breath of the Lord's on me because
Of how he has anointed me—then say
This scripture has been well fulfilled today.

Isaiah they know still in and out
And threats of God's vengeance they flout

Resound in his follow up lines.
But how can this man be performing signs?

They know after all is said and done
This man is a local joiner's son

And know all those kith and kin of his.
Ask who in God's name he thinks he is?

His work undermined by unbelief
Only a few sick here find relief.

Forced out, they have led him to a cliff
Above their hilled town, an east-west brow,
Intending to hurl him to his death.
He wonders at how they need to control
And how they did not know who he was,
Make homecoming prophets homeland prey.
He passed through their midst and went his way.

CAPERNAUM

Centurion, how do we plumb
Such depths of faith trusting from afar?
From east and west many will come
As those first kings shadowed a star.

Luke's telling says once you had built
A synagogue, fended for Jews,
And though you back Rome to the hilt,
You're seeking still, catching good news

Of one who heals, cures the unwell,
Of blind from birth given their sight
Who blab though told never to tell—
Lame walk, blind see, demons take flight.

No chronicler chose to record
What moves you more, leaving us to guess
Why you resend friends to say, 'Lord,
My servant lies home deep in distress'.

Your century's led by the nose,
Each will to yours promptly succumbs—
'I say to one go and he goes,
To another come and he comes.

'No need to come under my roof,
Unworthy, yet say but the word'.
Such sheer belief covets no proof—
Enough to heed all you have heard.

A WOMAN FROM SAMARIA

From a Samaritan, some wife who drew
Up water from a well, he asks a drink.
'You're asking me and you're a Jew?'

She blurts. 'If you just knew what I can give',
Hints Jesus, not knowing what she'll think,
'You'd ask for water that can live.

'I'll give you water that will surge and burst
Up to eternal life of sprung surprise'.
'Then give me some so I won't thirst'.

'Go bring your husband here along with you',
She heard him saying. She in turn replies:
'I have no husband to bring too'.

'You have no husband', Jesus now concurs,
'Because I know that seven husbands were
Once yours and this one isn't yours.

'So yes, it is all true what you avow'.
'I see', she dares, 'you are a prophet, sir!'
'The hour is coming and it's now

'It's not Jerusalem or Girizim
But in both spirit and in truth instead
All peoples worship him'.

'I know he's coming, that Messiah who
Arriving will proclaim all things', she said.
'I'm he, the one who speaks to you'.

But the woman left her water jar—
Much more than Nicodemus she's begun
To trust. Returning to Sychar

She asks Samaritans to 'come and see
A man who tells me all I've ever done.
He cannot be the Christ, can he?'

A ROYAL OFFICIAL

Cana again where he'd made their water wine.
Now an official whose son lay ill got word
Jesus had come from Judea; undeterred,
Though he well knew that his son might soon be dead,
Begged he be healed even on his dying bed.
'Won't you believe until I perform a sign?'

Did the official hear this as negative?
'Sir, come on down now before my son will die'.
'Go, he will live!' He believed Christ's stern reply.
Met by his slaves, there's good news about his son—
Fever had broken he's told that day at one.
This was the hour he had said 'your son will live'.

BETHZATHA

Stand up, take up your mat and walk.
We do not know the ill man's name;
Infirm for thirty eight maimed years
And no one before volunteers
To aid him though he's slow and lame—
Then comes the one who doesn't balk,

Asks if he wishes to be whole?
No help to bring him so again
Although he makes it on his own,
Each time he finds he's not alone—
There's someone there ahead just when
The angel stirs this water hole.

Stand up, take up your mat and walk.
At once the invalid is strong,
Takes up his mat and walks away.
All good and fine another day
But on the sabbath this is wrong.
The legalists begin to talk

And tell him how it's not allowed
On Sabbaths to lift up his mat—
But he who healed him told him to
Take up his mat, what could he do?
He who healed you? Who was that?
But Jesus vanished in the crowd

Till later in the temple where
He finds the man whom he made well
And warns him not to sin again.
But he reports all to the men
Who'd chided him. John doesn't tell
Why he informed. Was he aware

How naming Jesus prodded them
To challenge him? How could he dare
To break the law as they now knew,
Then say his father flouts it too?
The jealous and the doctrinaire
Foreshadow now Jerusalem.

SIGN

How many loaves have you got? Go and look!
A boy's two fish and five loaves Jesus took,

Then giving thanks he could feed all the mass
Who'd followed him and sat then on the grass

Arranged in groups eating bread there until
The food remains they collect still can fill

Twelve baskets though all were sure they'd run low—
Bread fragments' miraculous overflow,

Excess all four testaments fasten on.
Deep in their world Matthew, Mark, Luke and John

Would well recall how their God once had fed
His desert folk heaven-sent honied bread.

The scene is set for his last Thursday meal,
His bread with wine, tokens of death's ordeal.

Both old and new, generous two-way sign,
Five endless loaves lavish as Cana's wine.

DAWNING

His entourage a boatload rowing ahead,
While Christ has remained to pray,
But headwinds rise on battered oarsmen in dread
As three or four miles out they're hoping for day.

Like Job's stern God who trampled over the waves,
From Galilee's low coast
A figure walks the swell whose hurrying saves
Scared men full sure they've seen a watery ghost.

If it is you, my Lord, command that I come—
Poor Peter now strides out
On crests his newfound faith's unable to plumb
And stumbles into troughs of slithering doubt.

Take courage. It is I. Stop being afraid!
Played out the winds abate.
How little heed disciples truly had paid
When on few fish and loaves a multitude ate.

Have they not wondered who they follow before
Or thought who he might be?
As day now breaks and they are nearly ashore,
It dawns who walks in trust such turbulent sea.

BUT SOME OF YOU....

Many will baulk at the faith his words demand—
Some will now grumble or just softly leave.

Spirit gives life, else what's carnal is in vain—
What he is teaching so hard to understand.

Jesus is aware how some followers complain,
Though he has known full well who did not believe.

Former disciples begin to change their tack,
Wanting no longer to walk with him abroad.

Jesus asks twelve, 'Do you also wish to go?'
'Lord, then to whom can we go', asks Peter back,

'Since we have come to believe, are sure we know
You are the Christ and the chosen one of God?'

THEN JESUS CRIED ALOUD

Then Jesus cried aloud and said that who
Believes in me it's not in me that they
Believe but in the Father who sent me.

For I have come into the world to you
As light so everyone believing may
Instead of staying in the darkness see

The Father in their seeing me. If some
Do hear my words but don't heed what I say
I do not judge them as I came to save.

And who rejects the words with which I come
Have one who'll act as judge on that last day—
The words I spoke will judge how they behave.

O no, I have not spoken on my own
But speak for him who sent me, do his will.
Instructed by my Father's own decree

In what to say and what to speak, I've known
Eternal life is his commandment still.
I speak just as my Father has told me.

SABBATH

One day on the Sabbath as he walked through grain
Disciples who were hungry had unthinking fed
On ears that they plucked but the strict complain—

Just look how your disciples flaunt Sabbath code!
But Jesus responded have you never read
How David's companions with him hadn't toed

The line and when hungry dared to go inside
The house of God and then devoured the bread—
And priests work the Sabbath so God's magnified.

Desiring more mercy than a sacrifice,
The Sabbath's for man and it's not instead
That man's for the Sabbath and at any price.

I'm speaking of something that is greater than
The temple, so listen to what I've said:
The Lord of the Sabbath is the Son of Man.

THE SOWER WENT OUT TO SOW

God's kingdom is like—he will tell them once again—
But not quite sure they would ask him to explain,

To spell it out, to interpret, to expand
For stumbling men who still can't understand.

But then secluded, his parable seminar
On how the ground where a seed is sown may mar

Its growth: a roadside, a rocky place, a thorn;
How faith's seduced or when rootless, choked forsworn.

But why then speak in riddles and in clues?
The mysteries they have known the others refuse.

The walls have ears and many lay a snare—
His images test out the doubting air.

The long-grass powers-that-be still wait and spy.
Does all look yellow to every jaundiced eye?

They look but what can one-hued eyes perceive
Or who can hear what they can never believe?

A SAMARITAN

Just then a lawyer asks, 'What must I do
To be an heir to life's foreverness?'
'What says the law?' For Jesus knew he'd know—
'To love the Lord, heart, soul and mind too
And more, to love your neighbour no way less
Than your own self'. 'The answer that you give',
He's told by Jesus, 'is correct. Do so
And you will live'.

Self-justifying the lawyer tries once more:
'Who is my neighbour?' Jesus tells en route
To Jericho a man was robbed and left to die.
A priest walks by deciding to ignore
The dying man, a Levite follows suit.
But one Samaritan, unlike the other pair,
Anoints his wounds and in an inn nearby
Leaves him in care.

He pays the keeper saying as he leaves,
'Take care of him and then on my return
I will repay whatever more you spend'.
'Who's neighbour to the victim of the thieves?'
Asks Jesus of the lawyer now in turn.
'The one who shows him mercy', he replies.
Then Jesus brings this testing to an end—
'Go do likewise!'

FAITH

Unnamed woman who bled and bled although
Twelve years vesting whatever she owned she'd paid
In vain doctors to stay her clotless flow.

She knew how Jairus knelt and begged for aid—
A hand laid on his daughter and she'd rise.
Yet jostled by crowds this woman was afraid.

Amidst clamorous praise who'd hear her cries?
But she, choosing a tactic more indirect,
Glanced off fringes of God's human guise.

Did she brushing his hem in faith expect
A sign, silent, unseen, slipped in between
Expelled demons, dead he'd resurrect?

He knew someone had touched him though unseen,
He'd felt power seeping from him and could tell.
Now cured, trembling within she must come clean.

She'd touched Christ's cloak so on her knees she fell
Afraid, telling him why. He told her go,
Take heart, daughter, your faith had made you well.

MIRACLE

It happens during his withdrawal
To Tyre where seeking time apart
He thinks he left his fame behind.

A Greek shows up who will unload
Her cares. She heard how some describe
His miracles and though it's strange

For her a Gentile, she is on
Her knees explaining her concern:
Her little daughter is possessed.

But Jesus will at first say no—
Tells her to feed the children comes
Before all else and it's not fair

That we deprive our own and throw
To dogs our children's nourishment.
Disdained, entreating from below

Her answer humble yet aware—
'Beneath dogs too eat children's crumbs'.
'For saying that you may now go',

He'll say, 'The demon is suppressed'
And so the Greek on her return
Will find her daughter's demon gone.

Then was this miracle a change,
A turning out beyond the tribe,
A hairpin bend on wisdom's road?

As Moses once reversed God's mind
Did her retort stretch out his heart,
Allow that love encompass all?

CLEMENCY

Though in the temple only the night before,
Early this morning he has returned and tries
Now to instruct. A crowd has arrived to stone
Someone's false wife but firstly to test his views.

'Teacher, as she was caught in the act so then
Moses' law demands that we have to stone
Her. So instruct us, tell us what to do'.
Stooping he writes in sand, seems not to hear.

Anxious to catch him out they persevere.
Rising, he said, as this was a trap he knew,
'Who's without sin be first to cast a stone'.
Down on the ground he started to write again.

All of them slink away in ones and twos.
Jesus is left with her, she stands alone.
'No one condemned you?' 'Not a one', she replies.
'Neither do I condemn you, go sin no more'.

'Since we have come to believe, are sure we know
You are the Christ and the chosen one of God?'

WHEN?

Laying yet another snare
Pharisees try him again,
Asking Jesus to declare
How the kingdom comes and when?

'There's no watching it with care,
And no saying', he replies.
'Look, it's here or look, it's there!
In your midst the kingdom lies.

'Those preserving life find they
Lose their life, while others whose
Life is lost instead display
Life they gain in life they lose'.

ZACCHAEUS

Near Jericho when passing through
A short chief tax collector might not see
This Jesus from the crowd. He ran ahead,
But Jesus was aware just who he was.

On his arrival there he knew
How he climbed a sycamore fig tree,
So when he came there looking up he said,
'Zacchaeus hurry and come down because

Today I'll sojourn at your house'.
Zacchaeus hurries down the tree as he
Is glad to welcome him and celebrate.
Yet knowing tax collectors are impure

All who see it moan and grouse—
But just look how he has now gone to be
The guest of one who is a reprobate!
Zacchaeus stood and told him: 'To the poor

'Now half my goods I'll give away
And anything I gained by fraud or scam
I will return it all at any cost,
Repaying fourfold what those cheated gave'.

Then Jesus said to him 'Today
Because he's too a son of Abraham
Salvation's in this house—for it's the lost
The Son of Man has come to seek and save'.

A MUSTARD SEED

I bring you my son whom some spirits own—
A voice from the crowd cries for relief,

But Jesus all ears heard a doubting tone
O Lord I believe. Help my unbelief.

Disciples had failed, his rebuke is stern:
'How long am I here? Bring the boy to me!'

'Demon come on out, never to return'.
The demon obeys. Why then didn't we

Succeed though we tried, disciples now ask
In private again. Trust what trust can dare!

A mustard-seed faith tackles any task,
Shifts mountains at will either here or there.

All prayer is his plea crying for that son.
Across every age still this leitmotif.

The mountain will move. Nothing can't be done.
O Lord I believe. Help my unbelief.

ON THE MOUNTAIN

When Peter, James and John with him repair
To that peak, his face turns sun-drenched bright,
His clothes a dazzling white,
As Moses and Elijah come from where?

Are they visions, are they really there?
'O Lord', says Peter, 'let us tent you three'—
But suddenly they see
A cloud envelop them and from the air

A baptism voice then echoes to avow,
'This is my son in whom I take delight'.
And falling down in fright
They hear that voice demand they heed him now.

He touches, heartens them as they lie prone
And says, 'Get up and do not be afraid'.
Anxieties allayed,
When they look up there Jesus stands alone.

Such giddy heights for these three fishermen!
But they must keep what happened to this four
And tell no one before
The Son of Man is raised from death again.

God knows the depths of suffering yet to plumb.
One moment from beyond has broken through,
A blessed sneak preview,
A trailer for his glory yet to come.

GREATEST

'Who's the greatest in heaven?' disciples ask.
Does their question mask
Vying siblings determined to set the pace,
Sainthood jostling here for pride of place?

Those who want to be first are last of all,
At each beck and call,
Servant who serving others can humbly lead,
Mending what's still fragmented, tending each need.

Jesus beckons a child just to show them how
They must change, allow
Now their hearts be children, otherwise
They will never enter paradise.

Topsy-turvy, changed reality
They will learn to see—
Needless all the rankings they'd discussed.
Playful, free, foreseeing heaven's trust,

Children own the kingdom open-eyed
Still aglow inside,
Warmed in God's wonder, folded in awe's embrace—
Their angels in heaven see my father's face.

DEBT

Can parables shape our whole world view?
And yet it's only Matthew who
Recounts how heaven is likened to

A king once checking on his stock
That calls a slave who's so in hoc
He wants to sell him off. In shock

His slave now begs for time and goes
On bended knee till mercy flows
And he's forgiven all he owes.

But going out, although he's let
Clean off, he meets a slave in debt
To him, at once demands he get

What's owed him paid up on the nail.
His debtor pleads to no avail;
His cries ignored, he's thrown in jail.

Can flows of mercy so run dry,
That slaves forgiven can deny
Another slave the self-same cry?

But when his fellow slaves have heard
How he behaved, their feelings stirred
They tell their lord all that occurred.

The lord recalls his wicked slave
To ask him how he could behave
So ill. 'You knew how I forgave—

'As I when begged had pitied you,
Should you not show compassion too,
Forgive your fellow-slave all due?'

VINEYARD

Let Matthew tell the vineyard owner's tale,
A parable of heaven's endless yes
Ignoring all economies of scale.

He took on early workers who'd agreed
The daily wage with nothing in excess,
Enough to meet the average worker's need.

Four times throughout the day again a few
Still seeking work stood there with no success—
He hires them and pledges all their due.

When evening came and wages were disbursed,
Some men had worked one hour but nonetheless
Beginning with the last and then the first,

They all received a whole day's wage in turn—
For waiting and for labour full redress,
Which from the start of day all hoped to earn.

The first he'd hired expected some more pay—
Should they who worked one hour not now earn less?
They bore the burden and the heat of day.

The vineyard owner says, 'I do no wrong,
You've got your sum so why begrudge largesse
Rewarding those who haven't worked as long?'

'With what is mine I choose what I will do—
Beyond what's just and fair love's lavishness—
I choose to give the last what I give you'.

WIFE OF ZEBEDEE

Is the Salome present when Christ died
Who bringing spices found the empty tomb
The mother of both James and John to whom
He'd said it was his father who'd decide

When she the pushy wife of Zebedee
Had wanted Jesus to declare outright
That her two sons should sit one at the right,
One at the left, when in the long run he

Would come into that kingdom of his own?
For him her sons just left their father there
To fish with hired hands, it's only fair
That her own James and John should flank his throne.

But can you drink the cup I drink like me,
He asks—o yes, they can—they all replied,
But who sits where I don't myself decide,
Not even for the sons of Zebedee.

Her question irked the other ten of them
Yet every follower of his in turn
Will find that just like her they too will learn
His way will lead them to Jerusalem.

She'll follow Jesus to Golgotha's cross
And learn the answer to what she had asked;
Who wants to be the first must first be last,
Our sweetest gains lie in our own self-loss.

KING

    Near Bethphage and Bethany
    He's telling two
    To go into the village next to them
    And what to say if someone interferes.

    They're sent to seek a donkey out;
    As prophesised
    He'll ride into Jerusalem atop
    This yet unridden colt, a king unbowed.

    They find a foal that they untie
    And questioned why
    Responding just as he himself desired,
    They say, 'Because it's what the Lord required'.

    Aside the colt their coats are thrown
    To grace the throne
    They place him on and all along the way
    So many spread their cloaks in royal display.

    O blessed be the king who came
    In God's own name—
    The crowd began to sing in joy and awe
    In praise of all the deeds of power they saw.

    Some Pharisees among the crowd
    Say, 'Tell them stop'.
    But Jesus hearing them in turn replied,
    'If they stayed quiet, the stones themselves would shout'.

    He sees the city near and sheds his tears.
    'Jerusalem,
    If you could see what things bring peace to you,
    The things hid from your eyes that cannot see'.

TEMPLE

On entering this would-be house of prayers
He'll overturn their tables to expel
The money-changers, those who buy and sell,
Upset dove sellers' chairs.

But Jesus turns to quoting for them then
Those words that made a prophet's listeners quake—
My house is called a house of prayer; you make
Of it a robbers' den.

The blind and lame who came to him he healed.
When they saw the wonderous things he'd done
The chief priests and the scribes feel they've begun
To lose what power they wield.

As they have heard that children's cry first hand—
Hosanna to the Son of David,– they
Will soon in anger and their own dismay
Straight out start to demand:

'You hear what children say? You heard that phrase?'
'O yes', Christ says, 'But have you never read
From mouths of babes, from infants still breastfed
You have perfected praise'.

NEEDLE'S EYE

    A certain ruler asked Jesus how
    He'd surely inherit eternity—
    Reminded then what God's precepts allow,
    From youth, he replies, he'd kept each decree.

    'You still lack one thing he heard Jesus say,
    Go sell your possessions and give to the poor
    Come back then to me and follow my way'.
    We're told that he grieved but can't be sure

    If it's on account of how rich the ruler was
    That still he was balking at Jesus's advice
    As Gospels suggest, or was it because
    He didn't quite trust in some heaven's prize.

    More likely a camel through the needle's eye
    Than for the well-off to now enter God's realm—
    Jesus warns, as the ruler went on grieving by,
    To caution disciples his words overwhelm.

    The rich man now knew how all things he'd achieved
    Were not as he'd thought his God's favour shown.
    Perhaps it was not just his wealth he grieved
    But much in his heart he had always known.

QUESTION

Wanting to entrap him, have him say
Something that is so at odds
With the Roman law and clearly is

Grounds for prosecution, they began:
'Teacher, we know that you're sincere,
Neither do you care for any man

'Showing neither deference nor fear
You impart the truth of God's own way.
Tell us therefore as we want to hear

'Whether it is lawful then to pay
Tax to emperors or not?
Tell us what you think, what you would say?'

Jesus sees their malice, how they plot,
Try to find some trick they'll use;
So in answer he will ask them what

Coin they use to pay their Roman dues?
Brought then the coin he said,
'Show me this, explain to me now whose

'Coin this is, whose title and whose head?'
For all their traps catch as catch can,
Had they yet guessed just where his question led?

'Render unto Caesar whatever's his,
Unto God what things are God's'.
Hearing this amazed they went away.

TALENTS

Luke makes it clear it is just before
Jesus sets out for Jerusalem,
Where he knows well how they will condemn
Him to be killed, so he'll underscore

How his own kingdom will be postponed.
Jesus here tells them this parable,
Showing a case that's comparable:
Once there's this well-born man that owned

Land; when about to go off he called
Up and then gave—as of course he knew
He would return as their king—gifts to
Ten of the servants he held enthralled.

He on returning discovers how
They have all used every gift by then.
Do they behave like good businessmen?
How have they fared? What is earned by now?

One then came forward and said, 'Lord,
What I was given I've tenfold for you'.
'Well done, good slave, in small things you're true,
Charge of ten cities is your reward!'

Then comes another who has earned fivefold—
'Five other cities become your care'.
So comes a third much too scared to dare
Try to gain more is content to hold

Tight and enfold in a cloth his gift.
'I'm afraid, Lord, as you're so severe,
Reaping what others have sown'. In fear
He has just chosen a riskless thrift.

'Banking my gift would you not have grossed
Something worthwhile', the new king will say,
'What I gave him let you take away,
Give his one gift to the one with most'.

Those who earn more will be given more,
Those who don't earn will lose it all;
Doubting the light they with dark forestall,
Playing too safe they don't dare to soar.

SADDUCEES

The Sadducees who believe we don't transcend
Our sojourn here, that its end is where we end,

Have come to Jesus to try to lay a snare.
Now, Master, Moses has said as you're aware

If men die childless a brother must by right
Wed the widow and duly underwrite

His brother's line. But suppose then seven die
To every brother in turn the laws apply.

What if all brothers re-meet in afterlife,
Which one of seven claims her as his wife?

You err, warns Jesus, for all your priestly show
God's word or power in effect you do not know,

For God is God of the living and not of dead.
Like angels, though sharing in life the one they wed,

In resurrection unhitched their spirits dance
The light fantastic of heaven's vast romance.

SHEEP

The sheep on the right, the goats on the left—
The king will divide the sheep from the goats;
While sheep are rewarded, goats are bereft.
Old wisdom resounds in indirect quotes:

Who pities the poor, then lends to the Lord,
Whatever one gives the Lord will repay—
A proverb that's known and still strikes a chord
As Jesus describes the kingdom-come day.

Come you that are blest, for you all's prepared.
When hungry I'm one you were happy to feed,
When thirsty your drink you also have shared,
This stranger you welcomed, saw to my need.

When naked you gave me clothes that I wore,
Infirm it is you who came tending me,
In prison you eased the pain that I bore.
Inherit this realm, you're heaven's payee.

But, Lord, the rewarded start to inquire,
Just what could we do of any avail
Or how could we give you what you require
And when did we see you sick or in jail?

The King will reply I guarantee you
In seeing the weak it's me that you see;
The least of the world my kindred too,
All gifts to the least are given to me.

LAZARUS

(1)
When Lazarus of Bethany fell ill
His sisters, Martha and the Mary who'd
Perfumed with love the feet of Jesus till
The sober Martha had prepared the food,

Would send off word at once to him to say:
O Lord, the one you love so much is sick.
But then for two more days why did he stay
When all of them expected he'd be quick

To move to cure his friend? But Jesus said,
Explaining to disciples his delay,
He knew this illness would not leave him dead
But serve God's glory in a special way.

So two days on he said as they were near,
'Let's go into Judea then once more'.
'But Jews there tried to stone you and yet here
You're going back', they warned, 'What for?'

'Are there not each day twelve hours of light
And those who'd walk by day don't trip because
They see the world's own light but those by night
While walking come to stumble as there was

'No real light in them. Friend Lazarus
Has fallen fast asleep. I'm going now
To waken him'. Disciples wonder how
If he's asleep there's need for all the fuss.

They did not understand that he would wake
Up Lazarus from death. Were they naïve?
'He's dead but I am happy for your sake
I was not there so you may now believe'.

(2)
Among the four it's John alone unfurled
This story, heralding how though sacrificed
He will himself re-rise on that third day.
His raising Lazarus in turn then gives
The reason why Jerusalem was rife

With rumours of the power he could display.
Already many came to sympathise
And Martha heard that Jesus was now close,
Though Mary stayed at home she thought it wise,
Her brother four days gone to his repose,

To meet him now and kneel down at his feet—
'If you were here my brother wouldn't die,
But still God grants whatever you entreat'—
'He'll rise again' was Jesus's reply.
She said he would on resurrection day.

'But I'm the resurrection and the life,
Whoever believes in me though dying lives.
Do you believe?' This lets then Martha say:
'Yes, Lord, I do believe you are the Christ,
The son of God come here into the world'.

(3)
Back home she told her sister when alone
The teacher called for her
And Mary left at once, not on her own;

Imagining she went to see the tomb,
Consolers followed her,
But she had gone off to him to whom

She'll say, 'O Lord I know if you'd been here
My brother wouldn't die'.
Then she and the mourners wept. From sheer

Compassion Jesus much disturbed too cried.
'Where is he laid?' he asked—
'Lord, just come and see!' they had replied.

'He loved him so', some said, 'he had to cry'.
But if he heals the blind
Why then allow this man to die?

(4)
Outside the cave-like tomb where Lazarus lay
A boulder placed there blocked the entranceway.

When near the tomb he still was heard to groan
As he now told them to remove the stone,

'There'll be a stench', the warning Martha said,
'For, Lord, he is already four days dead'.

At his command they take the stone away—
'Believe and all God's glory is in play.

'My Father though by you I'm always heard,
I thank to show I am the in-flesh the word

'And that your sending me is not in doubt'.
Then in a loud voice, 'Lazarus, come out!'

The dead man exits clothbound head to toe
And Jesus says, 'Unbind and let him go'.

PLOTTING

Of those consolers who'd made sure to go
With Mary some trust, but spies and touts
Inform how Lazarus was raised to show

Belief in Jesus caused the dead to rise.
Chief priests and Pharisees will then conspire,
Ask, 'What to do? We have to realise

'If he goes on performing signs we'll see
That all believe in him and Romans will
Come here to ruin our holy place and we

'Will lose our nation'. 'Don't you understand
One dies to save a nation, all of us?'
Claims chief priest Caiaphas and so they planned

To kill him. John here lets the priest expand—
'Beyond the nation', reckons Caiaphas,
'Our God's children scattered through each land'.

The Pesach feast was near when by decree
The people came to temple so they'll still
Remember how their Lord once set them free.

They search for him in vain to their surprise—
'But do you think he'll come?' they all inquire,
'He may not come at all', a few surmise.

The chief priest warns, although he's lying low,
Whoever does find out his whereabouts
So they can seize him, must now let them know.

PASSOVER

John and Peter both were sent ahead—
They'd be shown a large room up a stair
And should make all the preparations there.
Jesus came and took his place and said:

'I desire to share before I'm killed
Passover's meal, I tell you now I will
Neither eat nor drink again until
In God's kingdom all will be fulfilled'.

Thanks given, he took and broke some bread.
'Here's my body given now for you—
To recall me this is what you'll do'.
Then when taking up his cup he said

To the twelve who sat around him, 'See,
Here's the cup that is poured out for you—
In my blood this covenant that's new.
Yet he who will deceive is here by me,

'He who will denounce me too has laid
Hands upon this table where we sit.
Though God's lamb is dying as deemed fit,
Woe to him by whom he is betrayed'.

Now what he'd said has set them questioning;
They begin to ask among themselves
Which of them it was could be this twelve's
Betrayer, which of them would do this thing?

JUDAS

His spirit distressed at what he'd foresee,
Ensuring his apostles now were prepared
He'd declared:
'There's one here among you who'll soon betray me'.

And Judas who listened knew that he'd sell
Underhand
His master with treason's kiss that he'd planned.
Had Jesus not chosen all his men well?

'Does he who'll betray you lie now in wait?'
Asked Peter who reclined by Jesus's side;
He replied:
'The one that I'll give what I dip in the plate'.

Though Peter had asked he must have been stunned
When he shred,
Immersed it then gave that dipped bread
To Judas who John said thieved from their fund.

The die has been cast, delay would be worse.
'Do quickly what you are going to do'.
But none knew
Why Jesus said this. As he kept the purse

Some thought that perhaps Jesus just might
Have said you're
To buy for the feast or give to the poor.
He took the dipped morsel, went into the night.

FOOT WASHING

His hour had now come, as Jesus was aware,
To pass from this world where having loved his own
Who were in the world, he loved them to the end.

He rose from their supper, stripped off and knelt with care
To wash and towel the feet, the flesh and bone
Of every disciple till he came to tend

To Peter who said to him, 'I will never let
You ever come wash my feet', but Jesus replied,
'Unless I can wash them you've no share in me'.

So Jesus then washed and wiped the sand and sweat—
A lord and a servant, rankings cast aside—
'What I now know you'll later come to see'.

Re-robed, as if in this foot-wash overflow,
He asks as he sits back down again to eat:
'But do you yet know what I have done for you?

'You call me your Lord and Teacher and that's so,
And still if as Lord and Teacher I washed your feet
So shouldn't you wash each other's feet then too?

'Now do for each other fully in accord
With what I have done in love for you, my friends;
My example is love for you made manifest.

'The servant is not greater than his lord,
The sent is not greater than the one who sends.
If knowing these things you do them you are blessed'.

FAREWELL

I still have much to say but this must do:
Although the world hates you as you'll soon see,
They hated me before they hated you—
They've neither known the Father nor known me.

When gone, recall things said before I went,
These things I did not tell you from the start.
But now I go to him by whom I'm sent,
Just telling you these things, grief fills your heart.

But yet it's best for you that I depart
For going away allows the Spirit scope
To guide you to all truth, my counterpart
The Comforter inspiring you with hope.

For all the Father has is mine now too;
The Spirit takes what's mine, shows all to you.

GETHSEMANE

It's here now to this place with his friends he'd gone
And asks they simply sit and pray;
Then leaves them to themselves, moving a pace away
To speak with Peter, James and John.

A stone's throw from these three now withdrawn, the son
Will kneel to pray his agony—
My father if you will take this cup from me,
Yet not my will but yours be done.

This garden of anguish where knowing all he knows
Anticipated griefs now flood,
Until bathed in sweat big as drops of blood,
The angel of acceptance shows.

Three times he returns, finds his disciples where
They'd stayed behind so they could keep
A watch; all are out cold, fallen fast asleep—
Why can't they stay one hour at prayer?

Their tired heads weigh them down, sleep is now all they seek—
But pray lest you should be enticed—
Although willing and wishing to heed their Christ,
The spirit keen, the flesh is weak.

If even they could stay an hour awake from fear,
But still none among them understands
How soon he'll be betrayed into those sinners' hands.
Get up! Let's go! My traitor's near.

BETRAYAL

Judas, who'll betray him, knows the place
Where by times with followers in tow
Jesus went and now alone would go,
Comes now with his double-cross embrace

To earn his thirty-silver-piece reward.
Soldiers from the priests and Pharisees
Come to find the man they want to seize,
Each with lantern, torch and readied sword.

Knowing what's to come, what plans they hatch,
Yet deciding he'd be first to speak,
He goes out and asks them whom they seek?
Nazareth's own Jesus they would catch.

'You will have my life at any cost.
I am he. Your men can go their way.
All's fulfilled and as the scriptures say:
None of those you gave me have I lost'.

Simon Peter strikes the high priest's slave,
Malchus, amputating his right ear.
'Put away your sword. His will is clear.
Shouldn't I drink the cup my Father gave?'

DENIAL

While Jesus faced the high priest's ire,
Warming himself by a charcoal fire

His chosen Peter lurks outside
And hopes he's not identified.

A servant girl who comes then stares
At him in half light and declares:

'But you were with that Jesus too'.
But he denies it and on cue

The cock has crowed. But then a man
Who half-knew him at once began

Accusing him, 'You're one of them!'
Afraid again they might condemn

Him too, 'That man I never knew'.
The foretold cock has crowed anew.

'I know you did', a third will say,
'Your accent is a give-away'.

As though in proof he cursed and swore.
The presaged cock has crowed once more.

Three times a faithfulness unkept—
And Peter went out and bitterly wept.

THE GOVERNOR

Though Pilate has asked if he is king of Jews,
First Jesus replies, 'You say that's so', then he
Stays quiet when some elders will denounce his deeds.
Still Pilate sees jealousy his challenge breeds.

Advised in a dream that this man lacked all guilt,
His wife had forewarned lest his blood be spilt.
He thinks that perhaps it may be Christ they'll choose
When offering a prisoner to set free.

'This Jesus is innocent, for what's he done?
I'll free you Barabbas', in despair he tried,
Choose him or Barabbas, 'So what should I do?
Say which of these two I should release for you?'

They know just at once who they are asking for,
'Barabbas we want!' the gathered crowd will roar.
'What should I now do with the Messiah one?'
The crowd shouts back, 'Let him be crucified!'

Still Pontius, the governor, deep down is dogged
By guilt, he knows this isn't justified.
But what of riots if this strife expands?
Before the multitude he washed his hands.

Absolving himself is he afraid or weak
And so gives a mob what he now knows they seek?
Releasing Barabbas he had Jesus flogged,
Then hands him over to be crucified.

TWO THIEVES

It's only Luke perceives
Such difference between the two
Beside Christ's cross the others say outdo
The mob in taunts, knows they before they die
Exemplify
A world of light and dark between two thieves.

One is poking fun—
'You're God's son then save all three'.
The other checks him saying, 'Can it be
You don't fear God when we now by his side
Hang crucified;
We're both so justly sentenced for wrongs done

'And here we pay the price.
He's not the one to mock or tease
As he has done no harm. Jesus, please,
Remember me when you are glorified'.
And he replied,
'Today you'll be with me in Paradise'.

LEGACY

When Jesus saw below his mother paired
With that disciple, one
He loved, there by the cross he had declared

His farewell legacy while hung above:
'Now woman here's your son'.
To him, 'Here's your mother'. Heirs of love.

'I'm thirsty', he cried out. To quench his drouth
They find a sponge they hold
Up on a branch of hyssop to his mouth.

Then from their sour-wined sponge a bitter sup.
'It's finished'. We are told
He bowed his head and gave his spirit up.

NICODEMUS

Part in search and part in half-belief,
Frightened to be seen by day
Nicodemus comes by night to say
'Jesus, Rabbi, signs you show
Mean that you're from God'– but even so
In-betweenness seems his leitmotif.

Almost like he says 'it's up to you,
Tell me all!' but Christ replies
Taking him so by surprise:
'There's no certain gained access,
No arriving in God's realm unless
From above you are reborn anew'.

'Old, how can we enter wombs afresh,
Somehow to be born once more?'
'Water and the spirit pour
New beginnings and create
Rises in God's kingdom's rebirth rate,
Nurturing the reborn in trust's own crèche.

'Don't be stunned by what I say, you see,
Winds will blow where they will blow—
Hearing them you do not know
How they blow just as they please
Just so for those the spirit wants to seize'.
Nicodemus asks how can this be?

Did he heed him? Or did he just not dare?
But he features once again
Risking telling elders when
They intend arresting Christ how he,
Though no prophet's due from Gallilee,
Thinks that Jesus needs a trial that's fair.

Now he's bringing in a final scene
Myrrh and aloes to perfume
Jesus lying in the tomb.
Same good man both rich and just,
Maybe cannot still completely trust—
Searching Nicodemus in between.

BELIEF

Still dark, it was Mary Magdalene
Who before day
Will find what she can't at all explain,
His tomb's closing stone is moved away.

To Peter and to the disciple whom
He loved, she'll go—
'They've taken the Lord from out the tomb
And where they have laid him we do not know'.

On hearing of this the two both raced
To where he'd lain
Though Peter is clearly well outpaced,
Yet seeing the tomb does not contain

The body, the loved one holds off
Till Peter who,
When going inside, sees the folded coif
Apart from the shroud. The loved one too

Believes when he sees that cloth inside
Which wrapped his head,
Though blind to what had been implied,
That he would now rise up from the dead.

THE WALK TO EMMAUS

Things hadn't turned out right
And two disciples sift the whole affair
While walking to Emmaus which they say
Lay seven miles outside Jerusalem.

Unrecognised now Jesus joins the two—
'What is it you're engrossed in talk about?'
They looked so sad as one of them replied,
'Are you the only one who doesn't know

About those things that have just happened here?'
'What things?' he asked them and they told him how
The prophet Jesus great in word and deed
Before both God and them was crucified.

They'd thought he would redeem them but he's dead.
This morning women saw the tomb but no,
He's gone. An angel standing by his shroud
Has told them he's alive but still they grieve.

'How slow of heart you are who can't believe
All that the prophets in their time avowed—
To reach his glory Christ must undergo
Such things exactly as the scriptures said'.

And walking on that roadway side by side,
From Moses on he showed them how to read
What prophesies foretold of him. But now
Emmaus where they're headed is soon near.

It's late. Though Jesus makes as if to go . . .
Invited for a meal he goes inside
And even now they haven't yet found out.
But then so unexpectedly they knew.

He broke and blessed the bread he gave to them—
Awoken by this gesture that third day,
They have recognised who had been there.
He had already vanished from their sight.

THOMAS

Thomas, who's called the twin, was absent when
Jesus had come and shown his hands and side.

In a locked room he'd said to them again,
'Peace to you all'. But Thomas now replied:

'If I do not finger the nail-pierced hands,
Poke inside his wound, I cannot trust'.

After eight weeks among them Jesus stands
Saying to Thomas, 'Finger my palms and thrust

Deeply your hand into my wound. Don't doubt!'
What's the need to touch or feel or prod,

Insert a hand? All faithlessness crossed out,
Thomas declares at once: 'My Lord, my God'.

Sceptical twin that all of us have been,
Nail marks and side-wound unseen, are we deceived?

'Thomas, you have believed because you've seen;
Blest who have not seen and have believed'.